"The book is highly readable and so absorbing that one would not stop without finishing it in one go. It will be a great hit all around the globe."

Jagdish Gandhi, Founder and Manager, CMS, Lucknow, India

"Oni Vitandham ranks among the handful of special human beings I have been privileged to know in my life. She is, as was Eleanor Roosevelt, with whom I once shared a day, truly humane.

"We have, to my profound gratitude, become friends over the years. I have followed closely her extraordinary efforts in establishing a Cambodian Service Center and School back in her home country. Her persistent belief in the fundamental goodness of mankind despite all that she has endured from mankind has been an inspiration to all who know her. May *On the Wings of a White Horse* now give testament to her courage and her humanity to the world at large."

David Brooks Arnold, Ph.D., Former Special Assistant to the President, International AIDS Trust and Former Director of International Relations, American Red Cross, President, PUAA the Foundation for Cambodia

"Oni Vitandham can tell the story from first hand experience. She is an eloquent, incisive and determined witness to the great wrongs done to her family and people. However, she is not vindictive. She simply wants the past uncovered so that reconciliation and rehabilitation can be achieved on the basis of truth. I admire her dedication. I agree with her judgment that without disclosure of past wrongs there can be no closure of continuing pain."

Honorable Justice Michael Kirby, AC CMG, High Court of Australia First Special Representative of the Secretary –General of the United Nations for Human Rights in Cambodia

D1225035

"I was a keynote speaker at the International Conference of the Chief Justices of the World Conference that was held in Lucknow, India on the theme "Enforceable International Law is the Need of the Hour." It was at that time that I was introduced to Oni Vitandham who grew up without parents in Cambodia, where she suffered horribly in the hands of Khmer Rouge that enslaved so many people. Now Oni has told her moving story, which has a powerful message concerning the problem facing thousands of innocent children worldwide. *On the Wings of A White Horse* is a story that will impact the reader and make a difference in the way they view their own lives. It is a story that finally reveals that one should never give up hope, and always continue to pursue survival, freedom and profound human love."

Sir James R. Mancham, KBE, Founding President of the Republic of Seychelles

"America continues to serve as a beacon of hope and a symbol of opportunity for the world. Oni Vitandham, raised in the jungle to avoid the Cambodian genocide, escaped and made her way to the U.S. through the refugee camps of Thailand. Once here, she managed to seize the American dream and make it her own. This book is an affirmation of what we stand for and what this country means to the world."

United States Senator Olympia Snowe

ON THE WINGS OF A WHITE HORSE

A Cambodian Princess's Story of Surviving the Khmer Rouge Genocide

by

ONI VITANDHAM

TATE PUBLISHING, LLC

Published in the United States of America
by Tate Publishing, LLC
127 East Trade Center Terrace
Mustang, OK 73064
(888) 361–9473

This book is designed to provide accurate and authoritative information with regard to the subject matter covered. This information is given with the understanding that neither the author nor Tate Publishing, LLC is engaged in rendering legal, professional advice. Since the details of your situation are fact dependent, you should additionally seek the services of a competent professional.

ISBN: 1–5988609–9–2

DEDICATION

To all the children of the world; may they never have to suffer the horrors of war, and may they always have a safe home filled with love.

To the future of Cambodia; may we create a democratic nation filled with peace and inspired by the heritage of Angkor Wat.

To all the people in the world who open their hearts and offer compassion to those who suffer, allowing victims of genocide to rise up against oppression.

To all those who have sacrificed so much, and especially those who have given their own lives, including my father and my mother, to free Cambodia from fear.

And finally, to all the Khmer families who remain in humble silence; we will instill the future of Cambodia with hope, love, and compassion.
We will create a place where all people can enjoy peace and realize their full potential.

ACKNOWLEDGMENTS

I offer my sincerest thanks to all those who helped make this book possible. To those who have supported, cared for, guided, and protected me, I offer my deepest gratitude.

I thank God for guiding me through difficult times and for showing me the extreme importance of love and compassion. I thank my godparents for teaching me humility and for their continuing guidance, which comes to me in the silence of my heart. Many thanks to all the members and supporters of Progressive United Action Association, the Foundation for Cambodia, who dug deep into their hearts and pockets, allowing us to open our Service Center in Cambodia. The Service Center gives children the chance to experience hope, find security, and gain an education upon which they can build their future.

I thank my editor, Joanne Kozovich, for believing in me and for her tireless efforts in helping me to find the words that reflect what I feel in my heart. God brought us together so that this book—a book that has the power to change the future of Cambodia—could be written. I thank Robert Lewis Simpson for his wisdom and for his gentle but firm mentoring. He showed me that effecting change meant taking action. I thank Senator Dianne Feinstein, David Brooks Arnold, Paul Sweet, Russell E. Lowe and Mary Miyashita for their work in ensuring that human rights and education become a part of Cambodia's future.

My deepest gratitude goes to Marin Nhean Has for providing a safe home for me and my daughter when times were difficult. I thank Channa Tan Ngov, and Paul Ke for helping in countless ways. I thank Michael Blasdell and all the PUAA staff for their extraordinary work toward bringing education and peace to the children of Cambodia.

To all my friends, who gave their time, energy, and commitment, I offer my deepest prayers and heartfelt appreciation. And I thank you, the reader, for taking time to listen to the voices of the millions of Cambodians who speak through this book.

There is one thing stronger than all the armies in the world, and that is an idea whose time has come.
—Victor Hugo (1802–1885)

Foreword

According to an old Cambodian proverb, "If you don't want the fish to rot, salt it. But if the salt becomes rotten too, then it is the end of the world." Thirty years ago, the world ended for many Cambodians. The salt of life became rotten. The unity and cohesion of national life was lost as killing and suffering of immense proportions overtook this small and once-gentle country. Families were split apart and in some cases completely annihilated as one Cambodian fought against another. One of the worst holocausts in human history next to Hitler's concentration camps took place in this tiny nation, where almost a quarter of the population died in just a few short years.

Although Cambodia's plight gained world attention in the 1970s, and Pol Pot's Khmer Rouge forces were eventually defeated, the problems did not go away. Today, Cambodia remains in a terrible state. Years of war have left the economy shattered, the social structure severely damaged, and the education system in tatters. Millions of Cambodians still live in desperate poverty. Hundreds of thousands of children starve and go without any education or proper health care. Outside influences pull the country apart for their own purposes, and the killing and suffering continue while the world fails to take notice.

This is the story of one young child who, like myself, survived the killing fields of The Khmer Rouge and escaped to safety in America. She lost all her family. She suffered abuse, sickness, and malnutrition as she fought to save her own life. She watched her friends and close ones slaughtered in front of her eyes. It is not a story that is easy to read, but it is a story of immense personal courage, remarkable in one so young.

For Oni Vitandham, however, the struggle did not end when she left Cambodia. Oni is a survivor of two different worlds: the killing fields of Cambodia and the city streets of urban America. Life was not easy for her as a poor, young immigrant. She faced many challenges as she sought to educate herself and make something of her life. In all cases, she showed amazing resilience and bravery in the face of obstacles that would defeat almost anyone.

Oni survived because she had a dream—a vision of putting Cambodia back on its feet, a burning personal desire to make sure that no other child, Cambodian or otherwise, ever had to suffer the way that she did. Her experiences gave her far more than courage and bravery. They taught her humility and compassion. They taught her honesty and a sense of justice. They taught her, above all else, that every human being has a right to live his or her life with the highest level of respect and dignity. As a result, she has devoted her own life to helping the people of Cambodia, whether they live in America or in our homeland. She has lobbied American Presidents and congressional representatives, written hundreds of letters to the United Nations, and has talked to whoever would listen. At the same time, she has helped young children in Long Beach, California, deal with drug abuse and pregnancy, assisted illiterate immigrants in filling out their financial aid forms, and fought for the rights of every Cambodian in the community. While doing all this, she has managed to raise a child of her own, as a single mother.

When Oni writes about her life, she is not just speaking on her own behalf. She is also speaking on behalf of the millions of Cambodians who will never get the chance to tell their story—those who died alone, afraid, and unrecognized. When she shares her vision for the future, it is not just her dream; it is the dream of all Cambodians to see their beloved country made whole again and Khmer culture once again vibrant and glorious.

Telling the story of those awful events in Cambodia is part of a necessary therapeutic process of recovery: First, recognition of what happened must come, followed by acceptance and understanding. This allows for forgiveness and a letting go, which is essential to healing the wounds of the heart. Once the wounds are healed, effective action can be taken to restore life.

Oni's dream is her plan for action, and she is working tirelessly to implement that dream for her country. When you read her story, I hope you will be deeply touched by her personal example of bravery, humility, and compassion. And when you read her vision, I hope you will be inspired to overcome tyranny and to strive to understand the people who surround you.

Dith Pran
Founder of the Dith Pran Holocaust Awareness Project, Inc.
Subject of the 1984 Academy Award-winning
feature film The Killing Fields

PREFACE

MY FACE AND MY NAME may not be known to you, but I was once an orphan who suffered horribly in Cambodia during the Khmer Rouge Genocide. As a young child I witnessed things no human should ever have to witness. Yet my story of survival is not unique—every Cambodian civilian man, woman, and child faced the same horrors as I did, although not many are willing to speak about it. However, I will not be silent. It is time the truth is told.

AS A CHILD, I saw my people starved to death, tortured, and brutally executed. To this day, these tragic and gruesome events remain clearly etched in my mind. When I close my eyes, I see my godfather taking his last breath, I see the bodies of infants and children lining the gutters, and I see the pain that was written on every member of Cambodian society during the insurgence of the Khmer Rouge. I will not try to forget the past, but instead I will turn these negative memories into something positive. My goal is to raise awareness of the appalling conditions that existed in Cambodia when I was a child and that still exist today. There is an extraordinary innocence present in the heart of each child, and I tell my story here for all those children who did not survive to tell their own. I was blessed to have met a number of remarkable people who helped me to survive through their selfless acts of kindness. In loving thanks to those people, I have devoted my life to doing the same for children in need around the globe. It is my greatest hope this book will help to increase the understanding of the plight of Cambodians in Cambodia, America, and throughout the world. Above all, I believe that there is nothing more important in life than finding and following one's spiritual path and destiny—for in the heart of every person dwells the spirit, and from the sprit comes action.

SURVIVING DEATH is a humbling experience. Coming to the edge of life reminds the human soul how fragile it is. I escaped death multiple times and am well aware of the fragility of my own body. Yet despite great adversity, I have continued to live, and within me lie the spirits of all those who suffered and died unnecessarily. These are the spirits that lead me into action. And so, I give you my story.

*May God create peace, prosperity, and love
in the heart of all human beings.*

When I first decided to commit the story of my life to paper for the world to read, fear crept up from deep inside of me. It wasn't a fear based on reliving the intimacies and horrors of a life that survived the killing fields of Cambodia. Rather, my fear stemmed from the language of the land that became my refuge and beloved home. As a Cambodian immigrant, I found that using the English language was, at times, a tricky endeavor. Nevertheless, I began to write from my heart, in whatever language flowed from my pen. The result is a story that I hope will empower other survivors of genocide and that will inform those who might not otherwise know about this moment in history that is often forgotten. Since America is the land of dreams, please allow me to dream that my broken English transforms into a beautiful message of ultimate hope, peace, and justice.

Surely there was a reason that I survived the same war that claimed the lives of 3.5 million others, including many of whom I loved and who loved me. It is for them and others caught in the midst of political turmoil that I look back into the heart of darkness with hopes of stirring the hearts of those who are willing to listen.

I have described these events according to the best of my memory. When I was a very small child in Cambodia, events often occurred around me under seemingly miraculous circumstances. As a child, I accepted these miracles without skepticism; in retrospect, I can see that some may find it hard to believe that what I say is true. To those who doubt the possibility of miracles, I ask that they try to see these events as I saw them—as an innocent child. I was only four years old when the Khmer Rouge invaded Cambodia and just eleven when I escaped to America.

This is by no means the entire story of what happened to me in Cambodia. I have described only the experiences that remain most vivid in my mind and that most accurately describe the atrocities that we, as a people, faced. The events related here are also the specific memories that have motivated me to lead the life I now lead.

During the traumatic years of my childhood and young adulthood, many generous individuals cared for me and in so doing, directly contributed to my survival. I am only able to describe a few of these people here, but I offer my thanks and have written this book in their honor. All of them are equally dear to me, as they were my family when I had none and my saviors when I needed to be saved. The lives they led and the experiences we shared are real.

Please note that when describing the people who served as temporary guardians to me, I use the terms Father, Mother, Aunt, Uncle, and Cousin. To address a non-relative in this manner is our traditional Cambodian way of paying respect to our elders.

Currently, I am corresponding via e-mail with the new King of Cambodia, His Majesty Norodom Sihamoni. With humble determination, I urge His Majesty to be a leader in the healing of our long-suffering Khmer people. I appeal to his sense of compassion and ask him to bring them peace and the security of democracy. I ask you, my reader, for something as well. Before you read my book, please bow your head in a moment of silence. I ask that you pray for the strength of the human spirit and for the strength of all humanity. I ask that you thank God for the people who have helped you to survive.

*There is a Cambodian legend that says a
white horse will come from the west to help
the people in their time of trouble . . .*

Survival in Two Worlds

CHAPTER ONE

July 1984

It was late at night, and we sat huddled together beneath the shelter of a large tree. The sky glowed with fire, and gunshots exploded all around us. The unseen fighting must have been coming from only one street away. Our neighbors were standing in their doorways firing guns toward the sky and occasionally waving them in our direction. We knew that death was coming for us, and this time we would not be fortunate enough to escape. We kept our heads down, our hands covering the backs of our necks to protect ourselves from the shrapnel that would inevitably rain down upon us. Explosion after explosion ripped through the air, reminding us that our time was short. We braced ourselves for the loud bursts that would not cease.

July of 1984 marked my eighth month of life in America. I had traveled there with several other Cambodian refugees as some of the few lucky survivors of the Khmer Rouge genocide. Many long years of fighting had destroyed our homeland, and we were thankful to be away from the killing and for the chance to start a new life in the United States. However, as immigrants in a strange land, we faced many unexpected challenges and understood very little about this new world to which we had come. We did not understand the language and nearly everything seemed foreign; it was impossible not to wish for something familiar to comfort us. We knew nothing of local customs and our everyday lives were full of confusion, yet we enjoyed lives of happiness because the hope for a better tomorrow was always in our hearts.

On the night of July 4, 1984, I was relaxing in the one-bedroom apartment of my godmother, Mrs. Touch. I had lived there with her and her seven children since coming to America, and after eight months we were just starting to get used to the plentiful amenities. It was the first time in our lives that any of us had a bed to sleep in and a bathroom with fresh water in which to bathe. That night, while the others watched movies in a language that they did not understand on the first television they had ever owned, I went into the kitchen to make popcorn. Mrs. Touch had purchased some of the dried kernels at the market, eager to try some new American snack foods. Being eleven years old and having been used to cooking my meals over open fires, I was unsure of how to operate the stove that sat like a porcelain beast in our tiny kitchenette. I called to the others, hoping they would show me how to tame the monster. One of Mrs. Touch's sons entered the room, like a knight preparing to slay the dragon. He made an elaborate show of inspecting the stove from top to bottom, hemming and hawing, before finally breaking up into laughter and saying, "You turn it on here, stupid."

He turned the knob on the stove to the highest setting. I watched as the electric burner slowly began to glow red. Although we had cooked many meals on this stove, it was still hard for me to comprehend the possibility of cooking without a fire.

I stood there in amazement, considering the vast differences between the country of my birth, whose ways of living now seemed antiquated, and our new home—a bustling, active, progressive country. Yet whether by fire or electricity, food still burns when cooked too long. I had neglected to notice that instead of popping, the kernels had burned to a dark black, and the kitchen filled with gray smoke.

I began to panic. "Smoke!" I screamed to the others. "Come, help!"

"Turn it off. Quick!" Mrs. Touch's son said as he ran into the kitchen. He turned the knob to the "off" position and removed the pan from the burner that still blushed with heat.

The popcorn was ruined, but as I fanned the smoke out a window, I couldn't help but smile at the laughter of the others in the living room. It was the laughter of those who had never before felt so carefree and were for the first time without fear. It seemed the devastation of a ruined batch of homemade popcorn was the worst thing we had to fear here in America.

Suddenly, gunshots erupted outside. I jumped back from the window as flashes of red and orange exploded in front of me. Instantaneously, the laughter in the living room ceased; no one made a move. Fear showed clearly in the faces of everyone present as the all too familiar repetitive crack of gunfire grew in volume and frequency.

As the explosions seemingly neared our apartment, the windows began to rattle and shake. I was taken back to a time when the sounds of American B-52 aircraft showered their missiles down upon Cambodia. When the noise of that bombing had ended, five hundred thousand Cambodian civilians lay dead at the hands of American forces. It seemed that every corner of every street had been destroyed. After the cessation of the explosions, the only sound to be heard was that of the Cambodian people crying out; they cried out for help, for mercy, and for God.

We feared that outside our apartment here in Houston, the story would be the same. We longed for the bombing to stop, but at the same time, we feared the devastation that would be left in its wake. Mrs. Touch was the first one to speak. "Hurry up!" she commanded. "Do you want a bomb to drop in your lap? If not, then get moving!"

We quickly jumped up and began to pack clothing and other belongings into the same tattered suitcases we had used when we were initially forced to flee from our homeland. We made sure to include water and food, knowing well what it meant to be starving and thirsty on the road of escape. As more missile-fire echoed through the neighborhood, we prayed aloud to God to protect us from harm.

We are surely in the midst of a major attack upon the United States, I thought. Fearing that the next explosion would destroy our apartment, we wasted no time. With our escape bundles tucked under our arms, we ran blindly downstairs and flew out the front door.

"Watch your step!" Mrs. Touch said. "Don't trip!" The darkness of night made it difficult to see our way down the stairs.

We searched for a place to hide from the shells that were now exploding in the air above us. Every color imaginable filled the sky as we took shelter under a large tree in front of our apartment building. Memories of the Khmer Rouge shelling our refugee camp in Thailand were still fresh in our minds, and we were sure that the killing of innocent people was about to begin again. The threat of encroaching death caused us to hold our breath while we held on to each other. We were under attack in a strange land, whose shadows, with their infinite darkness, held the memories of an unforgotten terror that waited patiently to envelope us.

We glanced furtively at our neighbors' homes and saw many of them outside, holding guns and waving them in the air. Some of them gestured toward us. We expected them to run at us, as the Khmer Rouge soldiers had with their red and white sashes flying, and kill us as we trembled beneath the sycamore. But they turned their weapons away from us and pointed them toward the sky. These Americans, bold and powerful, began to shoot at the heavens. I believed that by shooting at God, they meant to show that they had the power to kill us at anytime. We hid beneath our tree, waiting for a savior that we feared would never come. We had nowhere to go; we could run, but where to? It seemed that the eruptions of color in the sky carried on for as far as we could see. We remained huddled on the ground, horrified as we watched adults and children laughing in the face of the death and destruction that was headed their way. The smell of smoke and cordite in the air convinced us that the war we had known so well had finally come to Texas.

I shook in fear as some of our neighbors moved toward us. As they neared, I prepared myself for death.

"What are you doing? The fireworks won't hurt you. You don't need to hide," one man said calmly.

"War!" Mrs. Touch shrieked. It was one of the few English words she knew, but it was a concept she understood well.

His face softened. "There is no war. It's Independence Day." He pointed to the sky. "Those are just fireworks. They're just for show. For fun."

We did not understand the meaning of his words and continued to be fearful. A little Hispanic girl with pigtails came over and grabbed onto the hand of the man who had spoken to us. She carried with her a small stick that erupted with white sparks from one end. She extended her arm toward me, and I retreated in horror. I had seen children fight the battles of their parents in Cambodia, and it seemed in America children were destined to become soldiers as well.

"It's okay," the girl said. "Take it."

She smiled and held out the stick for me to take. On impulse, I reached out and grabbed it, eager to take the weapon and use it for my own protection. But as soon as I had it in my hand, I sensed its harmlessness. I watched as the sparks it emitted fell upon my hand and forearm, but I did not feel them.

"It's just a sparkler," the man said.

The sparks died down, and I was left holding a tiny and charred piece of kindling. I became incredibly confused. *What about the bombs overhead?* I thought. I pointed up to the sky and looked at the man plaintively, hoping he could help us understand the chaos in the sky.

"Fun. It's just for fun," he said slowly. "You're safe. You can go back home."

Safety was something we had never experienced, and our faces clearly showed our disbelief. He tried to explain it in a dozen different ways and to the best of his ability, but we could still not fully comprehend it all. We had learned that when unsure of what the consequences of our words would be, a single phrase was the safest thing to utter. So our only response to him was, "We say no English."

He chuckled at our ignorance. As he laughed, I began to relax. I couldn't believe that we were still alive and that this man seemed to pose no threat. No buildings had been destroyed, and instead of crying, all we could hear was laughter and music coming from the nearby apartments. The explosions above us seemed to be happy and harmless ones. Their colors and shapes began to bring out a sense of delight in me, and slowly the fear they had initially evoked dissipated. I was overwhelmed and began to laugh along with our neighbor. My laughing angered Mrs. Touch, and she gave me a dirty look and hit me hard over the head.

"What? Can't you see?" she said, pointing up at the sky, unwilling to believe that we were not in the midst of a war.

I grimaced, but her strike didn't cause much pain. Even if it had hurt, I was too happy to care. We were free, and I was beginning to feel it deep within myself. We were in America, a place where the sky was filled with magnificent reds, blues, greens and golds, and we were here to stay.

The man returned to his family across the street, where they were sitting in lawn chairs and gazing up at the sky. We stayed under our tree, watching the fireworks with the others until they began to cease and the people in the street began to go inside their homes. We stood, looked at each other in confused confirmation of our survival, and then walked to our apartment in silence. The explosions above had ceased, but the other noises from the city around us—the blare of sirens and the beating of helicopters overhead—forced us into the shadows of our foreignness. We hugged the corners and followed closely at one another's heels. Darkness enveloped us. America had proven itself to be a very difficult place to understand.

Later that month, I attended summer school at a local church to improve upon my English. I loved being around the other children, although I was frustrated by our inability to communicate. But we shared the common language of giggles and laughter in which all children are inherently fluent, and I soon made my first American friends.

On the first day of school, our teacher said, "I'd like everyone to tell the class about their Fourth of July celebrations." When it was my turn, and since I spoke very little English, I drew pictures on the chalkboard and gestured to the class, doing my best to show how my fellow refugees and I believed the fireworks to be the start of a war. The children in the classroom laughed.

"Hush, children," the teacher said in an attempt to quiet them down, although I could tell that he, too, was amused by my naiveté. He said, "This should serve as a reminder to everyone how fortunate we are to be living in America and how we sometimes forget that people of other countries are not free like we are." I returned to my seat, my cheeks glowing with embarrassment. He then began to speak to the class about America's independence. He told us about the men who wrote the Constitution and the political impact of the signing of the Declaration of Independence. Though I could only understand some of what he said, I understood enough to know that I was extremely lucky to be here in this classroom, in this city, and most of all, in this country. As he talked, I looked around the room and wondered how many of the other children really understood what it meant to be in America. I silently thanked God for the chance to experience life without the constant fear of being hunted and killed.

CHAPTER TWO

The Cave

*I remember riding on his back as a little girl. It
was as if heaven had gently transformed him into
a winged, white horse and I was being carried into
the heavens with him as he soared. He was the old
soul of the Khmer Empire and I was the spirit of
the New Cambodia, ready to fly into the future.*

I was born in a jungle cave in the Kompong Speu province of central Cambodia. While pregnant with me, my mother was living in the
cave with friends of my father, in hiding from the communist forces that
wanted to see them dead. She died in childbirth—the apparent fulfill-
ment of a prophecy given long before. I have been told that before my
birth, my father spent long days alone in the mountains praying for the
miracle of a child. According to Buddhist tradition, this form of isolated prayer would allow a person to gain favor with the gods. However,
when his pleas for a child were granted, they came with a terrible condition: a Mahari Sei, a holy seer, told him that with the birth of their child,
he and his wife would come to make a great sacrifice. They prayed for
a healthy child and a happy life for their family, but the prophecy was
to be fulfilled. The sacrifice, my mother's life, was greater than either of
them could have imagined. This was the irony of being in the favor of

the gods, and I became an orphan.

My birth name was Sisokhathini, and I have been told that I was born with an old soul. I was raised by Sarun and Cheata Voung Tan, but I knew them simply as Father and Mother Voung. Although he lived, I did not know my real father. He had arranged for the Voungs to raise me, for reasons I was too young to understand.

On occasion, other adults would visit our hidden home in the jungle. Sometimes I would sneak up behind the cave walls and listen to their intensely whispered conversations. There was one man in particular, distinguished and handsome, who would bring news from the city. Despite the serious demeanor he carried with him, he would often glance in my direction and let a smile escape from his lips. He took time to play with me and taught me words in Khmer, the beautiful language of Cambodia. When he wasn't playing with me or speaking with Mother and Father Voung, he would pace back and forth in a pensive mood, deep in thought. He was very handsome, with the soft, broad facial features and full lips typical of most Cambodian men. He dressed in dark green army fatigues and wore a white scarf that was the symbol of his army unit—the white was a symbol of the purity of heart with which he and his brother soldiers fought. It was believed that good spirits were wrapped inside the scarf to protect the wearer from harm.

I would pretend that he was a horse, and he would carry me on his shoulders through the tall grasses of the clearing outside the cave. He tossed me up to the sky; it was the picture of childhood innocence. Together, we chased the many different brilliantly colored butterflies that hovered around us while we played among towering trees and the rushing sound of distant waterfalls. We were very happy and laughed a lot together; I remember him tickling me and sometimes tears would moisten his eyes as he gave me a hug before leaving. He would tell me he loved me and I would put my face against his cheek, breathing him in. He would squeeze my hand with a touch that was delicate, yet powerful.

Mother and Father Voung called him Prince Chan and there were stories that he had married a princess from the Sisowath family, a prominent and powerful Cambodian line. He was a Prince of the Royal Members and was a top commander in the largest group of Issaraks, a group that fought to limit the control of the French colonists over Cambodia, also known as Kampuchea. He took on the important and dangerous role of speaking publicly on behalf of a democratic Cambodia, despite the risks. Yet when King Norodom Sihanouk sided with Chinese and Vietnamese communists, he discontinued his support. Conflicts arose between him and other Cambodian Royal Members. He didn't agree with their views that communism would benefit the Cambodian people, so he separated himself from them.

Prince Chan was then retained by Japan to lead forces that continued to fight the lingering French colonial presence in Cambodia. He put his personal distrust of King Sihanouk aside, was able to ally with him, and together they were able to obtain Cambodia's complete independence from France. Despite the King's communist ties, he became an active participant in King Sihanouk's administration with the belief that he would be able to help strengthen the Royal Cabinet. When his efforts to promote democracy proved to be ineffective, he once again separated himself from the King and became the commander of a poor infantry brigade based in the jungles of Kompong Speu. He gained great popularity among both his soldiers and the local population by selling most of his possessions to help support the efforts of his regiment. It is with this small band of Cambodian soldiers who loved freedom that he fought against Pol Pot's Khmer Rouge forces until January of 1975, when he disappeared. No one spoke of him again, and it wasn't until two decades later that I learned Prince Chan was my father and that I was a princess.

When my mother became aware of her pregnancy, Prince Chan was caught in the middle of a war. He knew his life was in danger; to protect us, he had to leave us. The Voungs cared for my mother until her death and continued to care for me afterward. I have been told that she was part Japanese, which explains my very light skin and why I am often mistaken for being Vietnamese. She was known to have been very beautiful, sweet, and humble.

My mother and father made great sacrifices for the sake of a peaceful life for all Cambodians. My mother gave her life for mine, and my father sacrificed everything he had—his possessions, his family, and his life—for the liberation of Cambodia. He valued democracy, equality, and freedom, and he fought to protect the human rights and dignity of the Cambodian people while communism threatened from the North.

My father's story was untold to the public then, and it still remains in the darkness where history holds its secrets captive. Like many pieces of Cambodian history, his story was not recorded in any textbooks, nor was it revealed to the public. The details of my father's role as an advocate for a democratic Cambodia remains sealed. Until now, it has been an unheard mystery.

The Mahari Sei had also prophesied that I would spend my life in service to the poor and less fortunate, and I would help to bring peace back to my homeland. This message, passed on to me by Father Voung, is the only real connection I have to my mother and father, and it is something I hold very dear to my heart.

The cave we lived in was situated in a narrow valley deep in the mountains, which kept us cut off from the political tensions present outside the jungle. A swift-flowing river ran past the small opening to the cave. One had to crawl on hands and knees to enter our home, but it was a small inconvenience for the safety it offered. A large rock that was placed near the opening blocked the entrance from view. Inside, straw blinds prevented any light from entering or escaping, and burning bamboo torches provided illumination. The cave was divided into two sections: a larger cave at the rear where we lived, and a smaller entry cave in front. Heavy cotton curtains served as a divider between the two rooms. The temperature stayed warm during the day and cool at night, no matter the season. A small stream ran through both caves and the sound of water running over rocks and dripping from the walls was a constant accompaniment to the rhythm of our daily routine.

I remember a marvelous sense of peace that draped itself about the place. The rock inside had a pinkish tinge and a rough, granite-like texture, but the light of the torches reflected off the stream and cast a soothing green hue over everything. The fresh scent of life and renewal mingled with the sweet aroma of burning incense.

We dressed in simple clothes made from naturally colored cloth. I wore short silk dresses with ruffled sleeves and a sash around my waist. Mother Voung wore a long tunic over a traditional sarong, which wrapped around her midsection and reached down to her feet.

With no grounds for comparison, I never knew that our lifestyle was extremely primitive. We had little food, simple kitchen utensils, no medical supplies, and few of the skills necessary to survive in this manner. Father and Mother Voung were much more accustomed to the sophisticated city life that they had abandoned for me. Nevertheless, Mother Voung went fishing in the river or hunted rats, snakes, and turtles in order to feed us. She roasted these animals over an open fire until the flesh was charred and often tasteless. Sometimes she would beg for food in one of the nearby small villages that dotted the surrounding jungle, but there was never enough to eat.

I remember bath times very well. Mother Voung washed me in a big, tin tub and dried me with large strips of white cloth. I never saw the adults bathe; perhaps they used the river. Sometimes I was allowed to play in the stream that ran through our cave. I loved slapping around in the cold water, but if I drank any of it, the icy temperature made my nose run and my head ache.

Hunger was something I knew well, but I was never allowed to grab at food like the primitive child I appeared to be. Mother Voung always made sure I ate properly, sitting upright with legs crossed. A sharp pinch on the arm was the reprimand I often received for slouching during meals.

Like most children, I was restless, mischievous, and curious. So to keep me occupied, Mother Voung kept me entertained with games using twigs and small stones. She would sing my favorite story, "A Rabbit Wants to Eat Bananas," when she put me to sleep at night.

Once upon a time, there lived a rabbit who often watched a lady farmer pass his burrow on her way to pick bananas in the fields. One day the rabbit decided he wanted to taste the bananas, so he lay down on the path that the woman would return home on and pretended to be dead. As she passed, she saw the rabbit lying in the road and thinking it would make a very good addition to dinner, she picked him up and placed him in the full basket of bananas that was balanced on her head. As she continued to walk home, the rabbit, who was feeling quite pleased with the success of his plan, ate bananas until his belly became full and round. He then jumped softly and quietly out of the basket. The woman did not notice and kept walking. Finally, she reached her home and set her basket down. The woman looked in and saw that the rabbit was gone and the bananas were eaten. She had been tricked.

I would lie in her arms and listen as I drifted off into my dreams. She would kiss me, saying, "Good night, my daughter. I love you." When I was young I never thought it was anything more than a silly story meant to make me giggle. However, looking back, I realize it was laced with a much deeper meaning. In order to survive the life that lay ahead of us, we would need to be fast and smart like the rabbit of the story.

Mother Voung put me to sleep on simple white sheets with pillows made from rolled up banana leaves. Now when I put my own daughter to sleep, sometimes I tell her the rabbit story and sing to her, and I think of Mother Voung serenading me those cool evenings in the cave.

Many times, I have tried to formulate a picture of her in my mind. I would love to be able to describe her character and personality in more detail, but the world of a small child is a very simple thing. To me she was just a mother—-the symbol of love, safety, security and presence—not so much a separate person, but more an extension of myself. She was always very sweet and tender toward me, but at the same time there was a certain disconnectedness between us. I felt the same distance from Father Voung. I loved them dearly, but even as a child I knew there was something missing. I knew that although they loved me very much, they were not my real parents.

Even if I were to forget the sound of my father's voice and the gentleness of his loving touch, he would always remain in my heart. When I was small, I never considered the possibility of Prince Chan being my father. I felt secure when he kissed me and was so confident of his love that now it's impossible to see it as anything but the love shared between a father and daughter. Our connection was strong and infinitely compelling. It was the thing that was missing in the relationship I shared with my godparents.

The last time I saw him, he was standing under a large tree across the river from the cave. He had a particularly difficult time saying goodbye and I could see the optimism, strength, and disappointment clearly in his face. Only his determination could help him to overcome the obstacles that he faced in the political whirlwind surrounding Cambodia at the time. I know that it was he who taught me to be strong, to be fearless, and to devote myself to pursuing freedom for our people. Today my father visits me in my dreams and I believe that his ceaseless energy will never fade. I have sensed the presence of his spirit in the stillness of hummingbirds and the gentleness of butterflies.

We shared our cave with an old monk of impressive stature. We called him Lork Ta Sar (holy man) or Lork Ta Lek (hermit). Hanging curtains divided his living space from ours. He was an imposing figure, radiating a tangible aura of peace. He must have spent many years in silence and meditation, and I was always awed by his presence. His face was oval with wide eyes, bushy brows, and a pointed nose. His head was shaved on top but his hair grew long at the back. He wore white robes wrapped around his upper body over a long shirt and simple pants, and he carried two canes, one black and one white. From the respectful way that he treated them, both seemed to hold some kind of special significance, but what that was, I was never certain.

Lork Ta Sar spent his days meditating and praying to a large statue of Buddha, which dominated the main cave and watched over us with the serene smile of enlightenment. A carpet of flowers surrounded the statue and beautiful green cloth hung on the walls around it. He would go for days without eating while he prayed. No one was allowed to touch him or go near him during this time, which he spent asking Buddha to bring peace to Cambodia. Sadly, his prayers went unanswered.

Lork Ta Sar fascinated me and I was often caught peering inside his holy books. At times when he was not meditating, he would speak to me. I learned many things while listening to his deep voice, laced with wisdom. He taught me how to chant and pray in the Khmer language.

One day I overheard Lork Ta Sar discussing me with Mother and Father Voung. "Her destiny is to travel a different road," he said. "She will have to witness much suffering, but she is a child with a gift of peace. One day she will help bring that peace back to our country."

As a child of only four years, his words didn't mean much. Yet later in my life, I would meet a man who would help me to remember the power of Lork Ta Sar's prophecy.

Life soon took a dramatic and violent turn. Our peaceful existence was destroyed as the Khmer Rouge violence overtook Cambodia and found its way into our lives. In 1975, Lon Nol and his American-backed regime toppled and the forces of the Khmer Rouge, led by Pol Pot, took control. Initially, the Cambodian people rejoiced, mistakenly thinking that the war was over. They welcomed a new regime, one that promised equal rights for all and a return to a simple agrarian economy. When the victorious Khmer Rouge troops entered Phnom Penh, Cambodia greeted them as saviors and people danced in the streets and tossed flowers in the air. Within a few days, however, events took a chilling turn, and a systematic campaign of looting and violence began. Under the false threat of an imminent American bombing of Phnom Penh, the regime ordered that the entire population evacuate the city. Hundreds of thousands of people were forced to abandon their homes and their lives, taking with them only what they could carry or push in a handcart. Lines of people several miles long stretched out from the city and into the countryside, heading toward work camps where they were destined to be "reeducated" and prepared for the new life that awaited them under the new Angkar government—the life of a mindless peasant worker.

Determined to rid the country of anyone tainted by the "evils" of Western living, Pol Pot ordered the killing of all those suspected of participating in such evils. Those who were students, teachers, government workers, business professionals, doctors and anyone else who demonstrated a predisposition toward anything but labor, were executed.

Those who were guilty of these crimes of "self-believing" were encouraged to confess, and many did, only to be executed. Those who were laborers (or at least able to keep their "crimes" a secret) were kept hungry and in fear for their lives. Rural labor camps became the death camps of what would become known as the infamous "Killing Fields." Young children were indoctrinated with Khmer Rouge propaganda and taught to erase any feelings of love or obligation they felt toward their families. Children were trained to be spies and soldiers, and it was not uncommon for a child to condemn their own parents to death. It was a state of life in which no one was able to trust others and the only reality was Angkar, the supposedly perfect Khmer society to which everyone now was forced to dedicate their lives.

What began as a plan to return the country to a simpler life soon mutated into blatant genocide. An entire society was destroyed as millions of innocent Cambodians lost their lives for crimes that were as innocent as speaking English. It is estimated that perhaps as many as one third of the population lost their lives during the Khmer Rouge genocide. We did not know it at the time, but our humble existence in the cave was destined to come to an end.

The Khmer Rouge

April 13, 1975, was the first day of the Khmer New Year, a time to celebrate the spirit and beauty of a new beginning. It was a chance to once again live in harmony and spread love through the country. The New Year celebrations were a guiding light in times of darkness. There were music, dancing, gifts of traditional foods, and wishes for a future filled with the glory of peace and happiness. During this time, the community traveled in groups to magnificent temples to chant prayers for the strength to live according to the morals and values of the Buddhist faith.

The Khmer are an honest and beautiful people who carry within themselves a strong sense of forgiveness, and they viewed the New Year as a time to forgive and look forward. The celebrations ended after three days. The French presence in their country had been eradicated, and the people felt the peace of a fresh beginning.

On April 17, only two days after the end of the New Year celebrations, Pol Pot lead the Khmer Rouge into Cambodia and turned Cambodia's dreams into nightmares. That day, as usual, Mother Voung went to look for food in a nearby village. When evening had come and she still had not returned, Father Voung began to sense that the turmoil that had loomed outside for so long had found us. His concern turned to worry, and he decided we should leave the safety of the cave in order to search for his wife.

As we were preparing to leave, Father Voung asked me to take off a necklace that I always wore—an amulet engraved with my birthday and the names of my mother and father. It was crafted of bronze and had a light, greenish-black hue and a symbol of seven colors that represented my family's line. Although, at the time, I did not know the meaning of the markings on the amulet, I had been told by Mother Voung that if I ever needed help, I could show it and help would be provided. This gift was the only thing left for me by my parents, and even today I fondly recall wearing it around my neck with pride. I could not bear the thought of abandoning it.

When I refused to remove it, Father Voung began praying fervently to God. When I continued to refuse he began to yell.

"We are in great danger in the world outside this cave. There are people who would cause us harm if they knew who we were. You *must* remove the necklace!"

He had never before raised his voice at me.

"But Father Voung," I said, "I love my necklace, and Mother Voung warned me never to remove it. I wear it all the time."

Father Voung grabbed my hands, and as I sat before him he began to speak in earnest. As I listened, I realized that there was something very serious and of grave importance that compelled him to act the way he did. He said solemnly, "That necklace can cause harm to everyone around you. It is your duty to remove it." He hesitated, then continued, "I cannot take it from you, but I fear that I may be unable to protect you as long as you wear it." He looked at me with pleading eyes and said, "It is our future that depends upon you allowing me to throw it away."

It was with a broken heart that I allowed him to take the necklace. The stillness of the cave amplified our somber silence. As he held it, his hands began to shake and his face turned a pallid green; it was as if the reality of the situation that awaited us outside the cave was becoming clear to him. As we crawled out through the mouth of the cave, I felt like a part of me had been taken away. We walked to one of the waterfalls and then searched the shore for what he referred to as "the right place." I was heartbroken at the thought of losing my cherished trinket, but I did not resist. When he found the spot he was looking for, he took a deep, almost silent breath. After saying a quiet prayer he threw my amulet into the water. I watched it slowly sink to the sandy bottom. We were surrounded by two large mountain peaks, many fragrant trees and the waterfall, which overflowed with clear, fresh water. It was a place of breathtaking natural beauty.

He said, "The water is pure here. Your necklace will rest in peace."

I could not understand the harm in wearing a necklace, and so I prayed that God would bring it back to me some day.

We searched for Mother Voung through the night and into the early morning. I held his hand as we pushed our way through the foliage and followed the narrow paths that lead to the village, and when my four-year-old legs grew tired, he carried me. By the time we finally arrived at the village outskirts in the midst of the jungle, eight miles away from our cave, we were exhausted from lack of sleep. The village was a collection of small, rudimentary bamboo huts with dilapidated straw roofs that were raised off the ground by roughly hewn wooden poles. We could see young soldiers squatting on their haunches in the square, smoking cigarettes and talking amongst themselves. They were dressed in black cotton, pajama-like clothing with red and white checkered scarves tied around their heads and waists.

Those scarves are like Prince Chan's scarf, except red, I thought. Black rifles rested on their laps or were slung over their shoulders, and many of the soldiers seemed to be no more than teenagers. They had captured about twenty villagers and had imprisoned them in what appeared to be a newly constructed, makeshift Khmer Rouge killing camp.

"There she is," Father Voung whispered as he spotted his wife among the bound prisoners. "Hide here in the trees while I go to Mother. Do not make a sound," he instructed.

"Yes, Father," I whispered. But before he could leave me, the soldiers were somehow alerted to our presence and rushed over to us with their guns drawn. They grabbed hold of Father Voung and threw him roughly to the ground. I watched as he put up no fight and tried to explain to them that he had meant no harm. The soldiers did not listen. They shouted as they put a gun to his head, then beat and kicked him savagely. He was sweating and shaking with fear. Begging for his life, his hands were pressed together in supplication. I was terrified; I had never experienced violence like this before and until now could never have imagined one human inflicting so much pain upon another.

The soldiers did not kill him, choosing instead to bind his hands behind his back. My first impulse was to run, but I was too afraid to move. Standing very still, I looked over toward the bamboo grove where Mother Voung was blindfolded and gagged. She was sitting in the mud with her hands tied to a bamboo stake behind her back, crying and quaking with fear. The terror that emanated from her being caused strange and powerful emotions to come over me. Suddenly, all that mattered was that I get to her.

God give me strength, I prayed as I started to crawl toward her. The soldiers remained distracted by their new prisoner and did not notice me as I inched toward the grove. I was a small and thin child, and I was able to easily slip between the bamboo stalks from the rear. The moment I reached her, I could sense her pain and fear. I began tugging at her blindfold and chewing on the jute ropes that bound her hands. The ropes were thick and coarse, and they cut into my gums. I kept at it, knowing I had to do whatever I could to get Mother Voung free. I chewed on them with such determination that several of my young teeth cracked and my fragile jaw broke. However, I felt no pain while chewing and only hesitated once as I felt blood begin to run down my chin.

I was naïve to believe that I could tear through the ropes, but a strong sense of purpose kept me going. I could taste the rope—at first it was harsh and dirty, but as it became soaked in the blood from my mouth, it became sweet as sugar on my lips.

After gnawing for what seemed like hours, the ropes finally broke and Mother Voung was free. The union between our spirits was powerful, and I was overcome by a sense of calm with the final snap of the fibers. We crept about twenty yards along the edge of the grove, where we were able to see that Father Voung had been thrown into the far corner of the bamboo. The soldiers had apparently lost interest in him and had wandered back to the huts. We approached him in silence, but as we attempted to free him, the other prisoners begged to be freed as well. Their pleadings attracted the attention of the guards and our attempted escape was stopped by a hail of gunfire. Bullets ripped through the mass of prisoners and Mother Voung was struck three times in the shoulder and twice in the stomach. She collapsed to the ground, her face twisted in agony. Bright red blood spurted like crimson water through her hands as she clutched her belly. It mixed with dirt and sand, forming a thick, foamy pool around her on the ground. The soldiers began to beat her, pulling her hair and kicking her repeatedly—on the head, shoulders, stomach, everywhere—as she lay bleeding to death. Father Voung and I watched helplessly as they gouged out her eyes with their bayonets. I cringed as she screamed for mercy. Her blood was everywhere and the other captives looked on with terror, as I did. The soldiers went wild, pushing them to the ground and smashing their heads in with the butts of their rifles. It was sickening. Brutal violence overtook everything, and the air became thick with the smell of blood and fear.

Hot tears streamed down my face as I grabbed hold of the torn and broken body of my godmother. "No! Not my mother!" I screamed. Her blood stained my white dress, and I cried for God to save her. It was of no use. Her wounds were too severe and she would soon bleed to death. I did not know what to do. The soldiers continued to strike her as I held her, but I could not bear to leave her side. With all her remaining strength she reached out and pushed me away. Her bloodied eyes became still and her body, limp, as she gasped for her final breath.

The momentum of her push sent me reeling toward Father Voung and as we reached for each other, my ears were filled with the horrific sounds of gunfire and death. The systematic bayoneting and shooting of everyone in the clearing filled us with terror, but Father Voung and I could not close our eyes; we were forced to watch as if in a waking nightmare.

It seemed as if time had stopped. As we watched unimaginable acts being committed against our gentle people, I thought to myself, *O God, I do not want to let them die!* I wanted to run and help them all, but as a child I could do nothing. I felt an empty, sick feeling in my heart, for up until that moment I had known nothing but love and kindness in the world. My reality had melted into a pool of blood at my feet.

We stood there, frozen in fear, until the sting of pebbles and rocks kicked up by poorly aimed bullets began to strike our legs. Amidst the chaos we ran, leaving Mother Voung's lifeless body behind. There was no time to say goodbye; there was only the frantic energy of running away. Bullets flew at us from every direction. Huge plant leaves wavered and stalks of bamboo splintered and exploded right before our eyes as bullets passed through them. The air vibrated around us as if filled with hummingbirds, and I wished that I had wings to fly away as we darted through the jungle.

We ran for what seemed like an eternity, motivated by horror and dread. We were chased by two soldiers who fired whenever they caught a glimpse of us through the brush. We did not stop, and eventually one soldier gave up; the second continued after us, but only half-heartedly, shooting wildly in our direction with a handgun. When he ran out of bullets, he ceased chasing us. Father Voung and I disappeared behind a thicket and plunged deep into the jungle.

We did not stop to eat or sleep, determined to put the danger as far behind us as we could. Above us, tall trees swayed in the wind, and on the ground the jungle was dense and steamy with moisture. We pushed through thick undergrowth that lashed at our faces and stung our cheeks. Our ears rang with the screeching of monkeys, the chirping of birds, and the shrieks and squeals of other small animals, as well as the rapid beating of our own hearts. Every sound warned of imminent danger. It was a divine miracle that we had managed to escape.

The humid heat was oppressive, and we were consumed with the constant fear of being captured by a Khmer Rouge patrol. I rode on Father Voung's shoulders; his body quaked beneath me as we stumbled forward. His breathing was labored and uneven, and he was very weak. Physical and emotional shock kept us silent for the majority of the time. We focused on nothing but putting as much distance as we could between the soldiers and ourselves.

As we lay in hiding, I blamed myself for the death of Mother Voung. It was I who had alerted the guards by attempting to free her. I had believed that I could save her, but in the end, I was the catalyst for her condemnation. I had only wanted to help the captives in the camp, but my reckless actions had caused their deaths. The injuries I received to my jaw caused significant damage, and with no way to treat my injuries, I was in a tremendous amount of pain. Father Voung was bruised and bloodied, but remained stoic. He tried to explain that the soldiers had killed our people—not me—but in spite of his consolation I would bear the guilt I felt that day for the rest of my life. Reflected in a mirror, a disfigured jaw and facial scars serve as constant reminders of Mother

Voung's horrific death. Sharing our tears of sadness, we waited in the bushes for hours. Father Voung then placed me gently on his shoulders, and we began our journey for Thailand, where we hoped to find our refuge.

Battambang

Father Voung's plan had been to cross the border into Thailand, but we soon discovered that Thai soldiers patrolled the area, preventing anyone from crossing. Anyone who was caught trying to pass over the border was shot in the head and left to rot on the side of the road as a warning to others who would try to cross. So instead we headed for Battambang, a regional center to the west of the Tonle Sap Lake in northwest Cambodia. Our arduous journey, which we made entirely on foot, lasted for about a month. We slept during the day and traveled at night in order to avoid detection. We abandoned our white clothes—they stood out too much in the jungle—and I left behind my blood-soaked dress. We made our new clothes out of banana and palm leaves that had been tied together. I was so small that one banana leaf covered me entirely. Whenever we heard a noise, we would freeze in place, imitating trees. Our organic clothing worked very well, but sometimes we were forced to stand still for as long as thirty minutes as soldiers passed by. The Khmer Rouge repeatedly shone their flashlights upon us, but luckily they were fooled by our camouflage; we had been blessed with God's divine protection. When the Khmer Rouge continued on patrol and we were once again alone in the jungle, we would continue to stand still in case any soldiers had been left behind to guard the trail. While standing there, allowing our disguised bodies to be absorbed by the wilderness, I would envision myself as a small bird, hiding in my protective nest from the predatory owls that circled above.

We passed over mountains and waded through rivers, keeping out of sight in the jungle. The floral canopy above us blocked out much of the direct sun, but the days continued to be hot and humid and the nights were wet and cold. Without proper shoes, it was hard walking on the thick undergrowth; my feet bled at the points where sharp branches cut into them and where blisters had formed and opened. Land mines were buried everywhere, hidden from view under the leaves. All that protruded was a small detonation spike, something easily missed among the large amounts of brush that littered the ground. We were extremely cautious of where we stepped; one mistake and you were dead or maimed. Each step we took was deliberately placed upon the ground, making our travel slow and tedious.

Our path was littered with the remains of those who had not stepped so carefully. Legs and arms, grotesquely separated from their bodies, were a common sight. I did not understand this carnage that was spreading unabatedly, and it was horrifying to see the dead. I soon learned that to survive we must remain hidden while constantly moving. I was angered by the soldiers who had destroyed my beautiful existence. I hated them and I began to fear nothing, least of all for my own life.

We would often climb to the tops of the tallest trees in order to sleep during the day and lessen our vulnerability to predatory animals and soldiers; two very different beings that were similarly fueled by a constant hunger for flesh and an unquenchable thirst for blood.

"For it is here," Father Voung would say of the trees, "that we are like monkeys or birds that find a place in the forest canopy to call home."

It was fun to think about myself as a monkey, and such imaginings were a welcomed reprieve from the constant anger and sadness that plagued my mind. Still, the reason for taking our lofty refuge was not for the fun of a childhood fantasy, but for safety. For it was high up in the trees that we could keep watchful eyes out for any movement below. The trees were inhabited with carnivorous ticks that attacked our flesh, but we were comforted by the fresh air and the fragrant flowers that surrounded us. We listened to the birds singing and once watched as a tiger sauntered menacingly below us, a threatening growl emanating from its throat.

When we did not sleep in trees, we would rest in flooded rice paddies; the long stalks helping to hide us from view. We covered ourselves in mud before sunrise and used the rice stalks as blankets to keep ourselves warm and safe. We sank into the marsh, letting only our noses protrude from the water. We lay there all day long while frogs jumped over our bodies, and snakes, attracted by our breath, would approach our faces with open mouths. Like the soldiers, they were always ready to strike. Leeches feasted on our blood. Workers from the Khmer Rouge labor camps and the soldiers who patrolled the fields often came alongside the dikes, within inches of us, but no one knew we were there.

We moved at night, guided along the overgrown trails by the owls that flew overhead. I felt like a displaced spirit, doomed to wander aimlessly. Even today, as an adult, I have trouble falling asleep when the darkness of night fills my bedroom. My soul remembers that at night one must remain alert and be ready to move.

We would patiently wait for the day to end. At nightfall, we would catch crabs, snakes, rats, turtles and frogs for food in addition to gathering whatever fruits, edible leaves, and vegetables we could find—usually pumpkins, corn or potatoes. I remember how we cooked snake flesh: after building a small fire, we would strip the skin off and curl the flesh around the hot coals to cook it. It was tough, chewy, and unsatisfying to our bellies, but we were energized by anything we consumed and so we ate whatever we could.

After a month of traveling, we finally reached the Battambang area. We discovered an abandoned, dilapidated hut on the edge of town, and we stayed there for awhile, keeping out of the way of the soldiers. However, late one day our vigilance lapsed, and while gathering food we walked directly into a Khmer Rouge patrol. They shoved their bayonets in our faces, the sharpened ends piercing our cheeks. They questioned our strange attire and asked us about our destination.

"We are from the mountains and are heading to Battambang to visit relatives," Father Voung lied. They offered to escort us there, and although we knew they were merely escorting us to one of the labor camps, we had no choice but to follow.

New arrivals in the village were forced to change into the black Khmer Rouge uniform and were housed in rows of small huts. They were simple bamboo structures, raised off the ground to keep snakes and other animals away. Father Voung and I were separated, and he was immediately put to work with the other adults tending to the rice fields. The work was harsh, lasting up to twenty hours a day, and no time off was given for illness, no matter how severe. If a worker hesitated to do his assigned labor because of sickness or any other reason, he was either beaten into submission or killed. It was hard, brutal labor, constantly supervised by armed Khmer Rouge soldiers, from which there was no respite.

Hard labor was a key element in Pol Pot's plan to subjugate the population. Everyone—men, women, and even children—were forced to do backbreaking work in the fields, digging ditches, and constructing dams and roads. Any sense of individual identity among workers was destroyed. All wore the same black uniform and androgynous haircuts—very short at the back and sides, and chopped off around the ears. Every day was a workday; there were no weekends or holidays. Food was constantly in short supply, and there was a severe lack of clean water and medicine. As a result of these meager conditions, many suffered and died from overwork, malnourishment, starvation, and disease. Some vanished without explanation and were never seen again; the only clue to their whereabouts being the sound of a lonely bullet echoing in the distant air. Days at a time would pass during which I would not see Father Voung. I would lay awake at night feeling empty and alone, waiting for him to return from work. My tears were my only company until he arrived.

During the evenings, we were indoctrinated with political propaganda. We were gathered in groups and encouraged to confess our sins of "self-believing" in order to join the spirit of the new state. Those who confessed were taken away and often never seen again. The Khmer Rouge preached that no one could be trusted, not even your family, and so all trust must be placed in the Angkar government. Everyone lived in fear of being reported as a "self-believer." Hardly anyone spoke to each other out of fear of having their words viewed as revolutionary.

Showing individual strength and determination was a crime, but to appear weak was equally deadly. The sick villagers that were fortunate enough not to be considered expendable were treated horrifically by the Khmer Rouge. One of their "remedies" for illness was to place red-hot coals on the stomachs of sick patients in order to purge their illnesses.

All this was part of an intentional campaign to create fear and distrust, to keep everyone weak and on edge. There was no one to turn to, no one with whom to feel safe. There was only an intense and all-pervading sense of isolation. We were surrounded by thousands of people—yet we were still alone. The Khmer Rouge planted seeds of suspicion in our minds, and these notions of doubt were fed by our fear. This feeling of distrust has never completely left the minds of the Cambodian people who suffered through this time of genocide. It has never left mine.

Everything beautiful had been taken from our lives. There was nothing for our spirits to rejoice in, no joy touched our hearts, and we had no family to comfort us. It was everything that life should not be.

Although the people of the camp worked hard and the yield of rice was good, they were not allowed to indulge in the fruits of their labor; the amount of rice allotted to each worker was miniscule. Each camp had a small warehouse in which to store the cherished grain, and the soldiers guarded it with vigilance. Every week, rice that was harvested by our camp was secretly moved at night to a nearby airport where Father Voung worked. He would watch as it was loaded onto planes bound for China, and he soon learned that the Angkar government traded the rice in exchange for money and weapons. He watched helplessly as plane after plane of our rice was sent to China while the Cambodian people were starving to death. Out of a desperation that was driven by a growing anger and an unceasing hunger, he stole a few small bags of rice from the warehouse to share with the workers at the camp. Shortly thereafter, Father Voung simply failed to come home. Just like that he was gone, becoming one of the many who disappeared with no explanation. A few days later, stories began to circulate that he had been caught and executed, his body probably tossed among the numerous other victims of defiance, thrown into some unmarked mass grave, or perhaps left to rot in an anonymous jungle clearing. China was fed on the blood of Father Voung.

Though the Khmer Rouge would have rather put me to work in the fields, my youth made me an inefficient worker. So instead, I was kept in a damp and dirty basement, a kind of crude day care facility, with approximately fifty other children. Although modern day care centers encourage learning and play, we were only taught hate and evil. We were made to believe that killing in the name of Cambodia was an honor, that the bonds of family were meaningless and empty, and that it was a sin to believe in anything but Angkar. We did not laugh. We did not play. We were not allowed to be children.

Only three pounds of rice were allocated per day to feed us all, and it was often tainted or spoiled. We were often sick with dysentery, fever, malaria, and measles, and the bodies of those children who died from their illnesses were often left to decompose in our basement until an adult worker was able to sneak out at night to bury it.

For several days I lay ravaged by malaria, sick and alone in the basement, wrapped in a dirty blanket and covered in my own filth. Flies crawled over my body and bit into my skin to lay their eggs. As the maggots hatched, they ate into my flesh, but I was too sick to move. Eventually, one of the women from a nearby hut visited the basement and took me in. Her name was Mrs. Vida, and I had seen Father Voung talking to her privately on occasion. She had been a doctor before the Khmer Rouge, and her husband had been the mayor of a small town. They hid their real identities for fear of being executed and struggled to fulfill their assigned roles as peasant workers. Yet if you looked closely into their eyes, you could see the anger that came as a result of their forced silence.

Mrs. Vida was very beautiful with soft lips and the full figure of a Cambodian woman. She was intelligent, honest, and kind, and cared for me as if I were her own. She never let me go hungry; any food she had she gave to me first, and then the other children, never complaining if she herself went without. I believe she would have sacrificed everything to feed a single hungry child.

"You have no idea what a very special child you are," she would tell me. I believed, in this new world of secret identities, she recognized who I really was, but had concealed my secret in her heart.

Another man, whom I called Chandra Sam, assisted Mrs. Vida with my care. In Khmer, the language of Cambodia, Chandra means moon, and like the moon, he had a rounded face and a gentle nature. He, too, seemed to know who I was, but never discussed it with me; perhaps

Father Voung had told him and Mrs. Vida before his disappearance.

The malaria had decimated my body; I was feverish, my hair had fallen out, and my belly was swollen from lack of nutrition. I lay all day on a rough bed on the floor of the hut, barely conscious, while he and Mrs. Vida were at work in the fields. In the evening, after checking in on me, Mrs. Vida would return to the hut she shared with her husband, and Chandra Sam fed me what little food he could find and mopped my brow with cold compresses, all the time mumbling prayers for my recovery. Slowly, I was nursed away from the edge of death.

Like Father Voung and everyone else in the camp, Chandra Sam stole food to supplement the meager rations we were given. The mounds of rice in the storage facility were a constant temptation for the starving workers, but the Khmer Rouge regarded theft as a crime against society, punishable by death. Many people were caught and executed for the simple crime of hunger. When a young girl denied that she had eaten some stolen rice, the guards slit her belly open so they could look inside her stomach for the evidence. When they found no rice, they pronounced her innocent of stealing, leaving her eviscerated body in the dirt.

Eventually, Chandra Sam was informed upon for stealing and early one morning four soldiers smashed their way into our hut. We were arrested and blindfolded with filthy rags. Pushing us forward with the barrels of their guns shoved into our backs, they marched us out of the village and into the jungle along with several others. Because of the blindfolds, we could not see the others, but we could hear their feet shuffling along ahead of us. Soon a sour, disgusting stench flooded our nostrils, and at regular intervals, a dull smacking sound could be heard in the distance. The soldiers forced us to a stop.

We could not imagine the location of our final destination. They removed our blindfolds, and we saw that we stood in an isolated field enclosed by small bushes and trees that obstructed our view of the village. We were surrounded by thousands of others who had been brought there ahead us. As confused terror filled our faces, they began to yell. "You want the bullet?" they screamed. I was overcome with panic when

I realized that we were going to be the victims of a massacre.

We were given a choice as to how we wanted to die. Our first option was a single bullet in the head, the second was to be doused in gasoline and set on fire, and the third was to dig our own grave and be buried alive. We did not respond; how could we? The field in which we stood was littered with decaying bodies covered with maggots and flies. Empty eye sockets stared at us from rotting skulls, the obvious cause of the terrible stench that filled the air. At the far side of the field were three large trenches, about twenty-five square feet in size and three feet deep, roughly dug out of the ground. Several lines of people headed toward these pits, their footsteps slow and heavy.

Soldiers selected people from the lines at random and pushed them forward, closer to the pit. As each person reached the edge, a soldier hit him or her on the back of their legs, forcing them to kneel, and then smashed in the back of their head with the butt of a rifle or a large hoe. It was a simple yet very effective method of execution, designed to save precious bullets. The symbolic use of the hoe, the basic tool of the agrarian life led by these people prior to Angkar, somehow made it even more sickening. The limp, dead bodies were then kicked into the mass graves. Skulls cracked and echoed across the field as each life was systematically taken.

As we were among the last to arrive that day, we stood near the end of one of the long lines. For what seemed like hours we moved slowly forward, marching to our death, our fear and revulsion increasing with every corpse we stepped over. As a child, I was more scared by the gruesome sight of the dead than by the thought that I was going to soon be one of them. It was a hot, dry day, and my mouth cried out for water to drink. Ironically, we were lining up in the same way that we did for food at the camp, only this time our only reward would be death. I began mumbling prayers, but salvation from God seemed impossible. Slowly we edged forward.

As we got closer, we could see that each trench was near full with blood-soaked bodies, twisted and smashed into crude positions. Among them were children and pregnant women, covered with black flies. Sightless, dead eyes stared at us from smashed skulls. The Khmer Rouge forced their victims to dig their own graves, and those who had dug these pits probably lay dead at the bottom, buried by their brothers.

It was an unreal situation—a ghastly nightmare that I could not wake from, no matter how hard I tried. A heavy feeling of hopelessness hung in the air and mixed with the nauseating smell of death. An expression of resigned inevitability and unbearable sadness was in the faces of those waiting to die. They had lost all hope—with their minds and bodies exhausted, their souls were easily defeated.

I began to cry.

"Be quiet little girl!" a soldier shouted at me. "Do you want to feel my blade in your side?"

I quickly wiped away my tears and became stoic. Chandra Sam hugged me and did his best to provide comfort, although he was shaking with dread himself. "Don't worry. If we die, we die together," he said.

As the afternoon sky filled with the oranges and reds of a beautiful sunset, we reached the edge of the mass grave and it was our turn to die. The soldiers seemed tired of the constant bludgeoning of the victims; I heard them complain of how sore their backs were from the repeated action of lifting and swinging their rifles. One soldier whistled to some others farther away and gestured for them to join him. They brought with them metal containers of gasoline. Only a few people remained in front of us and in a few minutes more we would all be dead, burned alive since the soldiers had tired of their previous labor.

Chandra Sam fell on his knees and begged the soldiers to spare us. He put his hands together and begged them to let us go, pointing out how young I was. They did not care. They doused us with gasoline and brought a burning tree branch toward us. We continued to desperately beg for our lives and amazingly, the soldiers relented. Perhaps our cries had reached the smallest remnants of humanity and compassion that remained in their hearts. Perhaps they were simply too impatient to wait for us to burn.

The few of us who remained were forced to swear our devotion to Angkar. We eagerly pledged our allegiance, willing to say anything that would keep us alive. Any sense of human dignity we had was long lost, and we knew that no matter how demeaning, full cooperation was our only chance for survival. Chandra Sam and I lay curled together in our hut that night, paralyzed with fear. It is impossible to describe how it feels when death comes so close and then suddenly recedes. Relief is obvious, but there is also bewilderment and confusion mixed with a sense of sadness and guilt that you survived while others did not. What little sleep came that night was due to sheer exhaustion and was riddled with nightmares.

The following day, the soldiers came to our hut and announced that Chandra Sam had been cleared of all wrongdoing. We could not bring ourselves to believe them, and their words did nothing to relieve our fears. They opened their eyes wide and pointed at us with strange, angry expressions on their faces. They called him Bang, which in Khmer means brother, and told us that since we had sworn our allegiance, we would be spared. I could not bring myself to trust their hollow and unfeeling faces, and I felt poisoned by their gaze. We feared that this was an attempt to raise our trust and confidence in order to make our execution easier. We stood still and silent, waiting for them to leave, and thanked God once they were gone.

It was not over. Later that day, they came for Mrs. Vida. The fear of discovery had always weighed heavily upon her, and she began to fall apart long before they came. She had begun to sing and cry hysterically, and she had lost all self-control. She mumbled to herself in a deranged way, babbling about her life as a doctor. I watched as a group of soldiers forced their way into her home. They strangled her, ripped her clothes, pulled her hair, and beat her. They laughed and felt no remorse or guilt at the suffering they inflicted. They used torn pieces of her clothing to bind her hands behind her back. Attaching a rope to her neck, they dragged her over splintered stairs and across the ground, rough with jagged rocks. Her naked body was covered in cuts and a trail of blood stained the dirt.

Gashes and welts appeared on her body as they whipped her. I could not help but feel as if I was watching Mother Voung die all over again, and the memories of her murder began to merge with the gruesome scene before me. Mrs. Vida called to us for help, but no one reached out for her. We knew that attempting to help her meant certain death from the soldiers' guns. The camp was crowded, but silent, as we stood by helplessly.

It was a lesson to us all—this was the punishment for self-believing. It made us sick to know that we had no choice but to commit our lives to the evil that was the Khmer Rouge. Despite everything they had already done to her, they were not finished. They took turns slamming her head to the ground until a dark red pool of blood formed in the dirt beneath her. Through all this, she remained alive, and with each impact she screamed and jerked in pain. Her suffering was great and their violence only increased. Finally, she ceased moving. Once they confirmed that she was not breathing, they shot her in the head. Her body stayed there in the street, swollen and bloody for a few days; we were not allowed to give her the dignity of a burial. I walked close to her and looked over every inch of her body, praying that God would punish all those responsible for her death.

I still recall that day vividly and with sorrow. I felt so helpless and impotent. There was no one I could turn to that could have saved Mrs. Vida, as there were no laws that protected us. If we questioned or spoke against the evil actions of the Khmer Rouge soldiers, they would execute us as dissidents. Hers was a cruel and humiliating death, simultaneously violent and degrading, and I will never forget it. During that time, I had no tears to shed. But today, twenty-seven years later, when I think back on her death, the tears flow and my heart grieves for her and all those like her who lost their lives.

In what must have been summertime, we were moved from Battambang to a nearby camp in District Four, where Chandra Sam was assigned to work building a canal. (Although we did not know it at the time, more people would be killed in District Four than any other area of the country.) The physical labor was rough on Chandra Sam and his health declined. I was still sick, and there was never enough food to help either of us recover. When he was no longer strong enough to do physical labor,

Chandra Sam ran the kitchen, supervising the preparation of the rice and thin soup that was served each day to the camp workers. To supplement this paltry diet, people ate anything they could find—insects, rats, mice, lizards, and scraps from the garbage—to stay alive.

One morning, two of Chandra Sam's helpers in the kitchen were caught stealing food. I was in the kitchen with them at the time and saw the soldiers force the accused thieves down to the ground. They grabbed one of the huge cooking pots full of boiling water, poured it over the screaming men, and then beat them with a large club until they were unconscious. They accused us all of stealing food and demanded that we come to them carrying our small bowls. There were about thirty of us in the kitchen, and with everyone watching they took a carving knife and hacked pieces of flesh from the unconscious men and tossed the parts into a kettle of sweet potatoes cooking on the stove. Legs, arms, and hands were cut into manageable pieces. They then filled our bowls and forced us to eat the soup that was tainted with the blood of our friends.

"Eat," they yelled, "or you will be killed!"

We closed our eyes and began eating, praying all the while for forgiveness. It tasted of blood and caused me to become violently ill. After eating, we were ordered to go to the fields to face execution. We arrived near a large campfire where more soldiers held some of the other workers. They called upon us one at a time, stabbing and then cutting out the livers of each victim. Five people died in front of me, hacked to death with machetes, their limbs severed and their livers placed on a skewer and grilled. A few unlucky victims remained conscious during the butchering and writhed in pain, screaming out like mad tigers.

Chandra Sam held me tightly in his arms, certain that this time, our death was imminent. I sobbed uncontrollably while the soldiers shouted for me to be quiet. One lunged at me with his knife, but Chandra Sam turned me away as it came near us. His alertness saved my life, but I was stabbed once in the belly and twice in the thigh. I was in an immense amount of pain.

The soldier wanted to finish me off, but his companion held him back. The killing of the two kitchen helpers and five of our other companions had diminished their anger, and they allowed us to leave. Chandra Sam took me back to his hut and bandaged my wounds in the best way he could. There were no proper medical supplies available to us, and infection was a serious danger. Chandra Sam decided that we must flee that very night, knowing how likely it was that our execution would be carried out the next day. Despite the risks, we managed to slip past a sleeping guard and under the cover of darkness, headed toward Laos.

CHAPTER FIVE

Laos

Our remarkable escape took us north of the Great Tonle Sap Lake and then finally, through the east. We walked day and night through the jungle, sparing only a few hours at a time to rest. My wounds made it difficult to walk through the thick underbrush, so Chandra Sam carried me on his shoulders. It was the rainy season, and the thick mud that formed on the ground sucked at our feet and hampered our progress further. We came across fields littered with the decomposing victims of the Khmer Rouge killings several times during our trek. It is hard to describe how many bodies there were. Huge areas of the countryside had become unofficial graveyards. We must have seen thousands of bodies during the two months or so it took us to reach Laos on foot. At one point, in order to avoid being discovered by a Khmer Rouge patrol, we were forced to hide in a rice paddy contaminated by human remains. We crouched down, submerged in the shallow muddy water as the soldiers crept by on the surrounding embankment. Floating in the muck next to the spot where my face broke through the surface of the water was a rotting human head, but I did not dare move. Lifeless eyes gazed at me from its smashed skull, only half covered with decaying flesh.

The threats of danger and death plagued us constantly. Land mines posed a threat wherever we went. Lakes and streams were often polluted, and it was hard to find water clean enough to drink. Food was scarce; we lived on roots and berries and whatever we could scavenge or kill. Chandra Sam applied a paste of herbs and water to my wounds and re-bandaged them with strips of cloth torn from our clothing, but several months would pass before they healed completely. He eventually replaced my ragged Khmer Rouge uniform with garments made of banana leaves and created shoes for me from cornhusks. I was once again a girl of the jungle.

As we headed further north into more remote areas, the immediate danger subsided, and sometimes we felt safe enough to relax a little. During these times, we composed songs to amuse ourselves, and Chandra Sam created whistles out of palm leaves for accompaniment. When the gravity of our situation weighed heavily upon us and made talking or singing difficult, he would just whistle softly as I sat astride his shoulders.

Around the middle of 1976, after a journey that lasted two months, we reached the Mekong River near the Laotian border. We had no choice but to cross it, however doing so seemed extremely dangerous. Chandra Sam held me up above his head, thrusting me toward the sky and shouted aloud, "Please God, help us." We waited for an answer from the heavens, perhaps even expected to be miraculously transported to the other side of the river, but nothing happened.

We did not know how deep the water was, so we walked down the murky bank to the river's narrowest point. I could not swim so I clung to Chandra Sam's back as he began to wade across. About halfway to the other side, his legs became stuck in the mud at the bottom. The water was freezing and the current was swift, and he struggled to keep his balance. I was terrified of being dropped into the waters and swept away. My hands were clasped tightly around Chandra Sam's neck, but my palms became sweaty and I began to slip. He felt me falling and grabbed my arms with one hand while clutching a bunch of strong reeds that stuck up from the water with the other. We stayed that way—trapped in the waters of the Mekong, anchored to the ground by a few small plants—until a fishing boat miraculously appeared in the distance.

"They will help us," Chandra Sam said, although we both knew it was likely that the boat was manned by Khmer Rouge soldiers. As it came closer, we could tell by the markings on the hull that it was a Laotian fishing boat, and those aboard were armed only with nets and fish bait. We waved to them, and they pulled up close enough that we were able to climb aboard the craft. They dropped us off about a mile up the river where we sat on the shore until our frozen muscles, warmed by the sun, were once again able to propel us toward Laos. By the time our clothes had dried, we had safely crossed the border.

We walked for what seemed like an eternity, covering nearly four hundred and fifty miles of Laotian territory. We eventually made it to the Houaphan province in the northeast region of the country. About forty miles from the city of Sam Nuea, the provincial capital, we came across a small, secluded village, nestled within the mountains. We observed the activity of the village from afar and Chandra Sam recognized the people.

"They are the Meo," he said, "descendents of the aboriginal Chinese. You can tell by their brightly colored clothing."

I was fascinated by their vibrant outfits of reds, oranges, and yellows. I wanted to see the fabrics up close, to soak up those living hues that were so different from the melancholic black Khmer Rouge uniforms we had been forced to wear.

Unsure of how they would respond to Cambodian refugees, Chandra Sam decided it best to keep our presence a secret. Using the same palm and banana leaves that had proved so useful to us before, we built a hut in the jungle a few miles from the village. For many months, we lived in complete isolation in the jungle.

Each day was an exact repeat of the one before, and it was hard to keep track of the passing of time. To provide a living, Chandra Sam chopped firewood and sold it in a nearby village market, a three-hour walk from our hideout. He tied the wood into bundles and carried it on his head for miles before finding someone who would give him a few precious pennies for his load of bark and timber.

To amuse ourselves in the evenings, we would sing, dance, and tell stories together. One story in particular helped me to understand the power struggle going on around us:

One day a rabbit went to drink water at a pond. On the way, he met a snail walking slowly along the path. The rabbit criticized the snail, telling him that he was slow and that it would take him an entire day to walk the length of the pond. These words upset the snail, and so he proposed a race to prove who was faster. If the rabbit lost, he would never again drink the water in the pond. The snail promised that if he should be the loser, he would leave his pond home forever. They both agreed to these terms and each looked forward to having the pond to himself. Knowing he could not beat the rabbit, the first thing the snail did was arrange for his snail friends to hide at different points around the pond. The race began, and the rabbit sprinted along the water's edge. When he was confident that the snail was far behind him, the rabbit called out, "Snail, where are you?" A snail somewhere ahead of the rabbit responded, "I am here." Shocked that the snail was ahead of him, he continued to race around the pond, this time faster than before. He called again, "Snail, where are you?" Another snail, somewhere ahead of the rabbit responded, "I am here." The rabbit kept running and kept calling out, but each time a snail answered from up ahead. The rabbit reluctantly admitted that he was defeated, never realizing that the snails had cheated and tricked him.

I was beginning to understand that the battle between Cambodia and the Khmer Rouge was similar to the one between the rabbit and the snail—both were struggles for power and control over the land. What I did not understand was how adults could resort to violence in an effort to gain power. But the potent effects of a bedtime story were stronger than any thoughts that floated around in my mind, and I would soon fall asleep in my godfather's arms.

When I awoke in the mornings, he would already be gone gathering wood, and I could not refrain from feeling nervous and defenseless. He would often return home very late and soon he began spending his time with a Laotian woman he had met at the market. I hated sitting in the hut alone, so I began to wander off in the evenings to investigate the village near our hut. Every so often, the villagers came together to dance and sing around a large fire. Their brightly colored clothing swirled around the firelight, and I was entranced by their movements.

I stayed hidden in the shadows, just outside the circle of light cast by the fire. Brilliant flames flashed their glow upon the smiling faces of the men, women, and children who danced. I can still hear them singing those songs that filled my soul with bliss:

> *We come to dance for fun,*
> *Each of us dance into the night,*
> *Be happy, forget the past,*
> *While we're young and trouble free.*

My soul longed to dance freely with them, but fear held me back.

One evening, as I ambled toward the village, I stumbled upon a hidden clearing where Vietnamese soldiers were executing the Meo villagers. I crouched behind a tree and watched, horrified, as the children were shot or beaten to death with clubs. Some of them were my age, only five years old, and some may have even been younger. Their bodies became bloodied rag dolls as they slumped to the ground, lifeless and empty. I picked up a large rock, wanting to throw it at the soldiers, but to do so would reveal my presence, and I had learned before that such an act would accomplish nothing except to add one more body to the pile. I let the heavy stone slip from my grip. Silent tears drifted down my cheeks as I turned and ran away, forced to abandon my unknown friends.

When I arrived at the hut, Chandra Sam was back and visibly disturbed by my absence. "Where have you been?" he asked. He became extremely agitated when I told him of the slaughter.

"Why are they doing this?" I asked. "I thought we had escaped the killing."

He remained silent, unable to find the words to explain something like this to a small child. Later I learned that the Vietnamese communist regime had territorial designs on both Laos and Cambodia, and they used war as a means to strengthen their position in both countries. The killing of children in Laos was part of the same campaign used by the

Vietnamese in Cambodia, their intent being to weaken the population thereby making the country easier to infiltrate. The Vietnamese also imprisoned many American soldiers in the caves of Sam Nuea, many of whom were never released.

Chandra Sam was confident that we were safe in our isolated hut, and we continued to live there unnoticed. But as time passed, he grew restless. Our conversations became shorter, and we did not sing or tell stories as often. He mentioned that he longed for an adult companion, an understandable desire after having been alone for so long with only a small child for a friend. He spent greater and greater amounts of time with the woman from the market, and in 1977, when I was six years old, he announced their upcoming marriage. The wedding ceremony was held in secret so as not to announce our presence to anyone in the village where she continued to live while we stayed in our hut. At night, she would sneak food to us—rice and vegetables and small amounts of meat. For a while, life improved, and Chandra Sam seemed content with our situation. He spent most of his time with her in the village, and I only saw her when she brought food to the hut.

Very gradually, she began asking seemingly innocent questions about us while visiting. She asked about Chandra Sam's past and would often wonder aloud why his daughter had such light skin while he was of such dark complexion. He admitted to formerly being a lowly official in the Cambodian government, but refused to talk about me, insisting only that I was his daughter. He soon started coming home drunk from his visits with his wife. Once, he was intoxicated for an entire week, and during one of his wife's visits began to brag that he had once acted as an officer in the Cambodian army. His behavior scared me; I knew it was not wise to admit to being a former officer, but I did not know how to stop him.

Blinded by his love for his new wife, he did not see that she was deceiving him. A very common ploy used by the Vietnamese was to train female agents to marry into suspected families in order to gather infor-mation. The Vietnamese government, like the Khmer Rouge, wanted to identify former government officials and intellectuals who were on their list for elimination. They often used drugs or alcohol to loosen tongues and expose secrets.

We were awakened at dawn by the shouts of Vietnamese soldiers. They destroyed our hut, bound us, and then threw us into the back of an oxen cart where Chandra Sam's wife waited. We were told that we were heading north for Hanoi and then blindfolded. The infamous Ho Chi Minh trail, once used by the North Vietnamese to transport troops and supplies to the battlefield in South Vietnam, ran through Laos and Cambodia near where we had been living. It was along this trail that we were now traveling. We marched for several weeks and the journey was slow and grueling. When I was allowed to ride in the bullock cart, it bounced over the rough terrain causing me to become bruised all over. We remained blindfolded during the entire journey, unable to see who or what surrounded us. During stops, they subjected Chandra Sam to many beatings and harsh interrogations. When he was returned to the cart, he sometimes babbled incoherently, as if he had been drugged. At one point, I overheard some of the soldiers speaking about him in Vietnamese. Although I could not understand everything they said, I was able to translate parts of their conversation.

"He is a high-ranking Cambodian official," one said.

"He got drunk and told that whore all about it," said another.

Vietnam did not reward the efforts of Chandra Sam's wife. When we reached the Vietnamese border, the officer in charge shot her in the back of the head. Her duty served, she was left lying dead by the side of the trail.

I came to learn that Laos had been taken and placed under Vietnamese control, just as Cambodia had been infiltrated by the Khmer Rouge. Vietnam's political games in both countries were sadly similar to the game played by the rabbit and the snail of Chandra's Sam's story; resorting to treachery, Vietnam aimed to gain control. We recognized this, yet Chandra Sam and I could do nothing but sit in the cart and wait for the game to end.

CHAPTER SIX

Hanoi

By the time we reached North Vietnam, exhausted and weak, I barely had the strength to sit up. It had been another long journey, covering over a hundred miles, but Chandra Sam and I had managed to stay together. We had survived so much that it seemed as if we had spent a lifetime together, not just a year. *As long as we have each other, we will continue to survive,* I thought. But once we reached the city of Hanoi, the Vietnamese soldiers separated us. I was to be sent to a juvenile prison somewhere in the city while his destination remained unknown.

We were only given a few moments to say goodbye. He got down on his knees in front of me and looked straight into my eyes. Placing his hands on my shoulders he said, "Be strong. Go along with whatever they say, but always keep the truth of righteousness in your heart." My body trembled under his hands.

He decided that I should take on a new name so that my true identity could not cause me any harm, and together, we chose the name Nga, which is Chinese for baby. The word carried with it the essence of innocence and purity, qualities he wished for me to always possess. He cried as they led me away, as did I.

The prison I was taken to consisted of several large canvas tents surrounded by barbed wire. There were about a hundred children housed there along with some older Laotians and Cambodians, and we were constantly guarded by unforgiving male and female soldiers. Discipline in the camp was sadistic and cruel. We were lined up outside our tents daily and made to bend forward in an awkward and humiliating position. Our hands and bare buttocks were then struck with bamboo rods.

Food was again scarce and many fell sick due to poor sanitation and lack of medicine. Fights would break out among the tiny prisoners all the time, especially when scanty food portions were served. Before, during, and after meals, we were subjected to communist propaganda and groomed for life as a soldier.

Because I had arrived with Chandra Sam, a known Cambodian official, I was interrogated repeatedly inside one of the tents. The heavy canvas walls trapped the heat and humidity inside the tent, and I often grew dizzy from the lack of fresh air. They questioned me for hours in Vietnamese, a language I barely understood, so I pretended not to understand them at all. They were seeking information about Chandra Sam, but I vowed to protect his identity as he had protected mine. I doubted he was still alive, and convinced that I would never see him again, I began to worry about who would look after me. I felt so alone and afraid; I knew this was not how life was supposed to be.

At night, sleeping on a rough burlap sack, I was plagued by nightmares in which I was killed as Mother Voung and Mrs. Vida had been. I could not rid my mind of the images of their unnecessary deaths: Mother Voung lying on the ground, her life spilling out of her, and Mrs. Vida, broken and lifeless in the dirt.

I was detained in the juvenile prison camp for several months. The soldiers continued to interrogate me, although with less frequency. Life settled into a routine of beatings, starvation, propagandism, and fear.

One night a female officer approached my bedside. Afraid that she had come to take me to be killed, I began to cry. She put her finger to her lips to silence me and gestured for me to follow her. Outside of the tent, there was a group of four inmates huddled together in the darkness. It was unusual that there were no other guards around.

"Do you want to leave this place?" she whispered in my ear.

I just stared at her, terrified that this was a trick. She looked around, taking stock of her surroundings, and then led us out of the camp. For two hours, we followed her through the darkness of a moonless night until we came to the waterfront. There, on the dockside, was another group of huddled people. One of them was Chandra Sam. This was no trick; we were being smuggled out of Vietnam.

My cherished godfather looked awful; his face was drawn and haggard, his body skeletal. He had trouble standing and was obviously very weak. I was astonished to see him, so I rushed over and threw my arms around his waist. He quickly discouraged me from making a fuss.

"You must be quiet, my child," he whispered to me.

In the water near where the group was standing, four small wooden boats, each one about the size of a two-man canoe, rose and fell with the waves. A long oar was attached to the back of each boat, sticking high up into the air. A large rock had been placed in the middle of each boat to provide extra ballast, along with some bread that had been wrapped in cloth. Chandra Sam lowered me into one of the boats, but as he began to step away, I grabbed his hand. I could not bear the thought of being separated again, and so I refused to let go.

"It's okay. I won't leave you," he said.

The female guard surprised me by stepping forward to embrace him. Tears glistened in her eyes as she pulled away, and he, too, looked very sad. She whispered a few words that were unintelligible to me, then quickly turned and disappeared into the darkness of night.

A sliver of moonlight reflecting off the water was the only thing that illuminated our escape. A fresh salt breeze blew across the surface of the water, creating small ripples that shattered the moonlight into irregular patterns. Our small flotilla of boats pushed off from the dock and made its way across the harbor, making as little noise as possible. The drivers placed their oars into the water with extreme gentleness, careful not to cause any unnecessary splashing. After the confinement of the prison camp, it was exhilarating to be on the open water, but it was obvious that we were in great danger, so our celebrations of freedom were kept to the silent leaps made by our hearts.

When we were a couple of hundred yards out from shore the sound of rifle fire and loud shouting split the stillness of the night. The bright beams of the soldiers' flashlights swept across the water as they tried to locate us. They fired several more shots, some of them hitting the top edge of our boat and showering our faces with wooden splinters. My boat had been the last to leave, putting Chandra Sam and I in the most danger. Fortunately, we were far from shore and cloaked in darkness, making us an impossible target. With Chandra Sam using all his remaining strength to row, we slipped around the headland toward the open water.

As we drove farther out to sea, the wind grew stronger and the waves grew larger. It was near the end of the monsoon season, and storms were still common in the region. The wind howled and roared, whipping up huge waves that tipped the boats side to side. Cold rain crashed down, soaking us. Salt water splashed over the sides as Chandra Sam held on to me. It was dangerous to face such seas in our small boats, but turning around was not an option.

Within a few hours, three of the boats had capsized. We could not see in the dark, but we could hear our fellow escapees scream as the sea tossed them around, sucked them in, and drowned them. By the time the storm subsided, only one other boat remained afloat besides ours. The four of us who survived were battered and seasick, unable to row another stroke. In the cold, gray light of dawn, the wind propelled us toward an unknown coast; it was possible we had been tossed right back from where we had come. Nevertheless, we longed for the safety and stability of dry land, and so we scrambled ashore and pulled the boats into the coastal jungle. Exhausted, we collapsed among the trees and slept.

Over the next few weeks, we floated down the Vietnamese coastline toward Cambodia in our small boats, moving only at night and hiding out on shore during the day. We survived on the bread the officer had given us and supplemented it with whatever we could forage. Storms continued to batter us as the monsoon season tailed off, and it was during one of these storms that we lost contact with the other boat. We never saw the people in it again, and it is my hope that they survived, but my fear that they did not. Chandra Sam had very little strength so I did most of the rowing, standing up at the back of the boat and thrusting and pushing the long oar, while he lay sick on the bottom of the boat. Even to me, a six-year-old, it was clear he was dying. Most of his days were spent in a state of delirium or unconsciousness, but in his few lucid moments, he explained the events that had occurred in Hanoi.

After we had been separated, the soldiers took him to some kind of underground dungeon where they beat, tortured, and drugged him.

"I worked with your father, and they wanted to find him through me," he said, "but they were never aware that you were right there, within their grasp."

The realization that my father was leading the fight to resist Vietnamese attempts to infiltrate Cambodia was shocking, but I didn't say anything, choosing to let him continue.

"The guard who smuggled us out from the Hanoi camp had acted as one of my interrogators. But at some point, she turned from jailer to sympathizer. When it became obvious that I was dying, she arranged for us to escape." He paused, took a deep breath and winced. Whether he was pained by his injuries, or by the thought of the punishment the woman inevitably faced for her actions, is hard to say. I suspect it was for both. I kept quiet for the rest of our trip down the coastline, using the time to whisper prayers for the woman and for my father.

Chandra Sam was determined to stay alive until we reached Cambodia. "If I am going to die for my country, then I will die in my country," he said.

After a nightmarish journey down the coast, we reached the Cambodian port of Kompong Som around the end of 1978, at the same time the Vietnamese government invaded Cambodia. By then, Chandra Sam was too weak to move. In order to reach the harbor walls, I had to fight large waves that raced towards the sandy shore. With what little help my godfather could offer, I managed to drag the boat up the sand and onto dry land. I tipped the boat on its side so he could roll out, but after doing so, he could not go any further; he had used all his remaining strength to get home. He pulled me close and spoke haltingly, his breath coming in short gasps.

"My time is over," he said, "and I am heading to a more peaceful world." He grasped my hand and squeezed it. "Always be true to yourself and fight for what you believe in." He paused for a moment and then continued to speak. "Please push my body back into the ocean after I die, so that it will not lie here for the dogs to devour."

I began to cry at the thought of having to do such an unimaginable thing. As I cried, his breath became increasingly difficult and blood began to ooze from his mouth and nose. He coughed his last breath, his eyes rolled back, and he was gone. I cried my prayers over him for a few moments, but knew that I could not stay on the shore for much longer. As the wind blew against my face and the waves crashed against the sand, I struggled to roll his body into the waters of the Gulf of Thailand. The last image I have of him is of his body, face down in the water, the waves gently rolling beneath him.

Whenever I feel sad or confused, I go to the ocean near Long Beach, where I now live. There, a large sand bar forms a sea barrier just as it does at Kompong Som. It is there that I think of Chandra Sam. He was a kind soul who cared for me through very trying times, saving my life on more than one occasion, although he had no obligation to do so. He taught me to dance and sing in the face of fear. In the midst of all the violence and hatred, he was a source of great, unconditional love.

Phnom Penh

With Chandra Sam gone, I was alone once again. I should have been scared, but his death left me with a strange feeling of peace. As I walked away from the ocean and into the streets of Kompong Som, I did not feel afraid. Armed conflict was raging as the Vietnamese army, backed by coalition forces, invaded and fought the Khmer Rouge for control of the city. Soldiers battled in every street and explosions rent the air in two. The empty shells of what had once been grand buildings littered the city and the acrid odor of cordite hung in the air. No one seemed to notice my presence as I wandered around, but eventually, a soldier grabbed me and hustled me over to the side of the street where I would be safe from the shooting.

His name was Sun, and he was with the coalition forces fighting to free Cambodia from the Khmer Rouge.

"What are you doing in the middle of the street, little girl?" he asked. His eyes were full of kindness, and a positive energy radiated from within him. "Where are your parents?"

With my answer came a wave of sadness. "I'm an orphan."

"Come with me," he said, putting his hand on my shoulder.

With international support, Vietnam invaded Cambodia and was now pressing the Khmer Rouge out of power. As the Khmer Rouge slowly retreated toward Phnom Penh, I traveled behind them with Sun and his military unit. He was a top official, as were the others we traveled with, but the others didn't seem to notice me. Their only goal was to get to

Phnom Penh, and as long as I didn't get in their way I was welcome to tag along. For several weeks, we walked or rode in bullock carts along the dusty roads that lead to the capital city, often having to stop and wait for the fighting ahead of us to cease before we could continue. It was winter, and the cold air turned the decomposing bodies on the ground a grotesque blue.

After a few weeks, we arrived in Phnom Penh. It was not safe for me to stay with him any longer since he would be in the thick of the conflict so I said goodbye, thanked him for his protection, and went on my own way. I heard gunfire coming from just a few streets beyond where I walked and constant explosions overhead caused the night sky to glow an angry red. Chaos now ruled the capital city. Since I had nowhere else to go, I huddled in the doorway of an abandoned shop and slept a fitful sleep for the remainder of the night. When I awoke in the morning, the nearby gunfire had subsided, but I could still hear the faint sounds of fighting coming from a distant part of the city.

I began to miss Sun. I had not been with him for very long, but he had been kind, and I longed for an adult's guidance. I contemplated trying to find him again, but I knew that he was in no position to take care of me. The pain of a stomach long too empty began to gnaw inside of me, and my immediate worries about being alone were replaced by a different concern—I needed to eat.

In the streets of the city, I begged for food but was unable to find anything that would cause the ache in my belly to subside. I had just about given up for the day and succumbed to the inevitability that I would spend another night without food, when I met a man named Mr. Tun.

"Where is your family?" he asked, looking around.

"I am an orphan," I said, the words slowly losing their effect on me.

"You can come with me and work at my house. I'll give you food. Come."

He lived in a large, run-down villa, and at first, I felt blessed yet again. It was originally white in color, but all the paint had chipped and peeled away and now large patches of gray cement showed through the crumbling stucco. The once-beautiful garden was overgrown and wild with weeds. Mr. Tun, like all my past guardians, seemed familiar to me in some way, but I thought it best not to ask any questions.

As an orphan, I was extremely lucky. While many other orphans had to survive completely on their own, I had been frequently cared for by adults who saw something in me that they thought was worth caring for. To this day, I do not understand why I was blessed with so many loving and caring guardians while others were not. I silently thanked God for providing me with yet another guardian.

The family had four children and several servants. Mr. Tun was light-skinned, short, and heavyset. He had a sweet demeanor that masked a more cruel side to his personality. There was none of the gentleness and kindness in him that there had been in my previous guardians, and I began to doubt that he cared for me as the others had. He never smiled, never placed a hand upon my shoulder in reassurance.

"Mrs. Tun will tell you what to do. You'll sleep with the other servant girls." And with that, he left me at the mercy of his wife, Tran.

She was a tyrant; cruel like her husband. She barked orders at us constantly with her commanding voice, rough and deep like a cannon. In return for our food and bed, we were forced to provide the family with extra income by pilfering jewelry and other valuables from abandoned houses within the city. I became an expert at breaking into locked buildings, but I adamantly refused to steal. For this act of insolence, I received regular beatings. I was not singularly treated, however, as the family was vicious to all its servants. The Tuns beat us often, and at night, Mr. Tun would come to our rooms and force himself on the other girls. When I witnessed him raping one of the servants, I knew that although it meant returning to a life of homelessness and hunger, I could not stay there any more. I would not lie in bed and wait for him to rape me, too.

A few days later, the Tuns left the house on an errand. I called the servant girls together and urged them to run away with me. I broke into the master bedroom, gathered all the jewelry I could find, and offered it to them. In this case, stealing seemed justified as I knew it would help to keep the girls alive on the streets, at least for a while. Only two of the girls had the courage to leave, so I divided up the jewelry between them, added rice for the journey, and sent them off, instructing them to go in different directions to avoid detection.

I decided to go to Angkor Wat, the ancient temple city built near the Tonle Sap Lake in the center of Cambodia. It had once served as the capital of the ancient Khmer Empire before being taken over by the Khmer Rouge and used as their headquarters. The Khmer Rouge had since abandoned it, and the devout had resumed making their pilgrimage to the ruins that remained there. I have no idea what prompted me to go to this ancient site. I only knew that a loud, clear voice in the back of my mind urged me to go. I set off walking, finding my way by asking for directions from people in the street. It is a two hundred mile journey from Phnom Penh to Angkor Wat, but I would travel any distance to escape the tyranny of the Tuns. I had a blue and red sarong tied around my waist, a striped towel across my shoulders, and nothing else except the strength and determination of a very experienced seven-year-old to carry me over the next two hundred miles.

The Vietnamese presence in Cambodia proved to be just as deadly as the Khmer Rouge to the Cambodian people. Every displaced refugee I met in the street looked tired, dirty, and distraught. Despite the fact that the Khmer Rouge had vacated Angkor Wat with the arrival of the Vietnamese, it was certainly not a safe place to be headed as it was still surrounded by land mines and sporadic fighting.

The road to the ancient city was strenuous and painful. I had no shoes for my journey, and after several weeks, my feet showed the familiar marks of walking barefoot for miles on hard, uneven roads. I was tired and my feet were sore, so I stopped to rest in an abandoned barn. I had no idea where I was, but it didn't matter. My spirit was already in Angkor Wat.

I fell asleep on the warm hay, but was roused in the morning by a cow that was licking my cheek, face, and nose. It was lying next to me, and its warmth made me feel safe, not scared. Her body was hard, solid, and somehow very reassuring. It is said that if a strange animal comes into a herd of cows, they will gore it with their horns and chase it away, but if another cow joins them, they will welcome it by licking it with their tongues. This cow was obviously prepared to accept me as part of its family. It is impossible to describe how much that meant to me at the time—that someone, even a cow, would offer me such affection. I stayed in the barn for several days while my feet healed, and I gathered my strength. I helped local villagers carry buckets of water in exchange for rice. In the barn with the cow, I was blessed with a few rare moments of warmth and companionship in the midst of the fighting and killing.

One day I heard yelling between the people who lived in the house that neighbored the barn. A woman inside the house screamed, "Somebody help me, please! Please help!"

I rushed over to her assistance and found her held at knifepoint by a man who was threatening to cut her throat. Her face was pale with fear and his raged with hatred. I had seen enough killing, and I could not stand to see it again. Determined to keep the knife from spilling this woman's blood, I screamed at the man to stop. Shocked by my intrusion, he turned to look at me. Noticing my size, he began to laugh.

"Go away, little girl," he said, "Go and play with your dolls."

The woman's face was filled with panic. "Don't leave, little girl!" She screamed. "Please help me!"

What can I do? I thought. *I'm just a skinny seven-year-old. I can't defend myself against this man.* Yet I could not leave this woman to be killed, either. I decided to stand firm.

As he turned back to his wife, I said, "Put the knife down, Uncle. We have survived so much. Please don't hurt her."

"Leave us alone!" he screamed, turning the knife toward me. My hands moved to the spot on my stomach where I had been stabbed by the Khmer Rouge soldier. Still, I stayed.

"I cannot leave you here to slaughter your wife like an animal. She is not an animal!" I said. "Aren't you tired of all the death we have seen? Why kill what has survived for so long?" I pleaded.

The muscles in his neck relaxed a little and he sighed deeply, dropping his head. He took his hand from around his wife's throat and let her go. She ran to me, grabbed me, and pulled me out of the house. Her husband did not follow, but I could hear him sobbing inside. She knelt down and wiped the tears from my eyes first, and then her own.

"Thank you, little girl. You know, he does not hate me. It's the fighting that he hates."

I nodded because I knew what she meant. It is hard to see such great quantities of death and devastation and not yield to violence yourself. I was afraid to face her husband again, but also afraid to leave her alone.

"Will you be okay?" I asked.

"Yes, child. I will. He loves me, but sometimes simply surviving is just too much to bear."

The cow looked sad as I knelt to kiss it goodbye. I took off on the road to Angkor Wat. I asked the others who were walking the same road as I, "Where are you going?"

Their reply was usually the same: "To Angkor Wat." I must not have been alone in my inexplicable desire to travel there. I followed them, although my feet and toes were once again rubbed raw. Although we did not speak, in the eyes of those who traveled alongside me silently, there was much pain and the deadening ache of anger. The quiet days of walking allowed for many hours of contemplation on the tragedies that had filled my life, but I kept the goal of Angkor Wat foremost in my mind and put all my energy into getting there. Amazingly, I never tired.

CHAPTER EIGHT

Angkor Wat

It was many weeks later, in 1979, that I arrived at the marvelous temples that comprise Angkor Wat. The nearest village was seventy miles away, and even though I had sometimes been able to hitch rides in bullock carts, by the time I got there my feet were skinned and bleeding. However, I forgot my pain when I saw the ancient temple rising magnificently out of the mist, appearing almost pink in the rays of the early morning sun. The beauty, majesty, and divine splendor of the temple shocked me. The size of the buildings alone was breathtaking. The wind seemed to blow through my soul, cleansing and rejuvenating it. I was unable to merely walk across the bridge, for what I saw moved me so much that I ran as fast as my injured feet could carry me. I approached the temple by the great stone causeway that served as its entrance and then quickly scaled the stone steps. I felt that this was where I belonged; I was safe and at home. I looked around and touched the ancient statues.

I spent days wandering alone among the ruins, soaking up the silent energy of the temple complex. Much of the stonework in the main temple had eroded naturally, but I could also see the evidence of damage from war and pilfering, the blasphemy of which saddened me. Bullet holes marred the stone walls, and the heads of several statues were missing or lay where they had fallen upon the ground. The statues of the apsarases, the celestial dancers who performed for the Buddhist gods in heaven, drew me to them. It was as though they spoke to me as I stood before them. In the Buddhist faith, a religious statue is not just considered a piece of carved stone, but a living being, an actual manifestation of the god it represents. In my mind, I could feel the suffering of the deities who were broken into pieces and discarded among the ruins.

I decided to sleep in Angkor Wat, to live there as though I owned it. It was cold at night, and all I had to keep me warm was my sarong and striped towel. For a bed I slept on a bare stone slab. Even so, I slept well and flourished in the peaceful environment.

When I woke in the mornings, there was food—rice and water—placed in bowls near me. At first, I looked at the food warily, wondering whether or not it was safe to eat; I feared that it might be poisoned by an unseen enemy. Yet soon my ravenous hunger won out, and I devoured it. The rice was soft and tender and was seasoned with something I can only describe as divine. The bowls were refilled every morning, but I never discovered who it was that fed me. The miraculousness of this occurrence somehow seemed natural in the exotic atmosphere of the temple.

I lived and thrived in this manner for a month before coming across an ancient tree that grew in a courtyard toward the back of the temple. Its huge, exposed roots climbed over the side of the building, as if the tree was animate and creeping slowly into the temple. Yellow leaves covered its branches, heavy with the dignity and majesty that only very old trees possess.

The ancient Cambodians had planted palms around the boundaries of their country as a form of territorial demarcation. By planting trees, the Khmer also believed that they were planting the roots of their nation. But when war broke out, the trees were cut down for their fruit and juice by those who refused to recognize their symbolic meaning. The Vietnamese had also marked their territory in a similar fashion with bamboo trees, from which they also fashioned sharp spears. These spears were used to kill the Khmer people while simultaneously claiming Cambodian land as their own. However, this lone tree in the temple courtyard was not a palm nor was it bamboo. It was a singular kind of tree, and it had somehow survived the chaos, and I felt drawn to it by a mysterious force. I prayed to God often upon the ground beneath its boughs.

Many people came there to pray, so I took it upon myself to act as caretaker of the temple and the surrounding area. I picked up any trash that people left behind and made sure everything was in its proper place. I swept the floor with a palm leaf. One day strong winds blew the leaves from the piles I had swept. The winds continued to gain strength until it was a struggle for me just to keep my balance. I sat upon the roots of the old tree for shelter, when suddenly it grew cold and I felt the pure water of a raindrop fall upon my head. This single drop seemed to penetrate my entire being, cold and powerful. No other rain fell from the sky, just that single drop. As I sat in the tree's shade, a sense of timeless peace and indescribable joy settled over me. I was safe and no longer alone; the tree was somehow protecting me. I felt as if I had existed there for centuries. As I sat, I played a game using the leaves from the tree, and when I tired of my game, I went to sleep. As I slept, I dreamt that this tree was my tree, put there for me as a gift from God.

When I awoke, I was startled to see a tiger sitting very near to me. My muscles tensed as I prepared to be attacked and eaten. It was large and powerful, but it simply sat there gazing at me with large eyes and a partially open mouth. It had a warm, comfortable look about it as it made soft, guttural growling sounds. I looked to the side of the tiger and noticed a large, black snake hiding between the stones. Initially, the snake had its mouth open and was spitting and hissing, but it soon settled down, making no move to strike. I sat there, very still, until my fear subsided, and I realized that both the tiger and snake had been sent there to keep me company. I was confident that they had some sort of divine power, for as the day passed, the tiger's face began to look almost human. After warming itself in the sun, the snake finally moved off. When the tiger noticed its actions, it, too, rose and moved off into the jungle.

As I remained seated and motionless under the tree, contemplating the presence of the animals, a bright light shined down upon my face. Unexpectedly, my thoughts became crystal clear. In that moment of clarity, I realized how important Angkor Wat was to the future state of peace in Cambodia.

Without thinking, I picked up a leaf and automatically began tracing the same symbol over and over again on my hand. At the time I did not know what it was, but later, I recognized it as the Khmer letter, sar. In the Khmer language every letter carries a deep spiritual significance. The meaning of sar is purity, integrity, loyalty, trust, honesty, faith, compassion—qualities that needed to be returned to the Khmer culture if it was going to survive.

I found myself wanting to spend more time praying for the return of peace and harmony to Cambodia, and I knew that I would eventually have to devote my life to this end. It may seem strange that a seven-year-old girl would have such deep thoughts, but it seemed very natural at the time. All I knew was what I felt in my heart. I began to lose despair and gain hope for a better Cambodia. As I continued my stay at the temple, often contemplating these thoughts, it gave me intense joy to think about the future. What had once seemed bleak and hopeless now had purpose and strength.

Eventually, I was filled with the desire to visit the jungle around the temple complex. I do not know why I wanted to go there, but my instincts were strong. Coming to Angkor Wat had definitely been the right decision, so it seemed that visiting the local area would also be a good idea. I was learning at an early age that it is always important to follow your heart and to let your soul guide you.

The immediate landscape around Angkor Wat was very green and dotted with palm trees. Further out, the land was more heavily wooded and interspersed with fields where people had once farmed. Land mines were everywhere making it unsafe to walk, especially at night because the triggers were not as easily seen.

During one of my many journeys through the Angkor Wat jungle, I saw a man heading toward the temple. He looked determined and was running haphazardly through the brush and foliage.

"Uncle! Look out for the mines!" I yelled to him.

He ignored my warning and continued to step without taking his eyes off the temple. He screamed when the mine exploded beneath his feet. I screamed, too, and ran to his side, barely missing a land mine trigger myself. My leg was cut from the sharp metal protruding from the ground, but by the grace of God, the mine did not detonate.

He was breathing heavily and bleeding from multiple wounds. I felt my clothing become warm as it absorbed his blood.

"You'll be okay," I said, trying to comfort him.

"No, I won't. This is my end. Look at my legs!" he cried, motioning to his ravaged limbs.

"You will survive. Let me help you to the temple." With my help, he was able to walk to the stone steps. He sat on one of the rocky platforms, but instead of appearing overcome by the pain of his injuries, he seemed to be rather calm and intensely sad.

"Why did you not watch the ground while you walked?" I asked, devastated by the ability of the Khmer Rouge to kill and maim even after they had been defeated.

"I had to get to the Buddha before anyone else," he said.

"To pray? There is no race to get there," I said.

He winced in pain. "One cannot live on prayers. I need food. The head and arms of the Buddha statue would have bought a great deal."

I was disgusted by his sacrilege. I was tempted to push him off the platform, to get him away from the ancient statue that he had planned to decimate for a few pounds of rice. It was not his to take. It belonged to the Khmer people.

"You would destroy this temple for food?" I asked, trying to control my anger.

"I'm not the only one. Look around, many statues have been sold. Who cares? They're just rock, but valuable rock. I need to eat!" he said, holding a hand over a cut in his thigh.

I turned my back on him, unsure what to do. I was disgusted by his actions, but still, he was injured and needed help.

"Little girl, you have no idea what it is like out there," he said, indignant.

This caused me to turn around. "I know what it is like. I have seen it, but that does not mean God has abandoned us, and we must never abandon Him!" I could feel the tears welling up in my eyes, and my face was hot with intensity. I walked away from the platform, leaving him there on his own. When I returned later, he was gone. I prayed to God, asking him to protect the injured man.

On occasion, monks clothed in saffron would come to the temple grounds to wander and pray, but I generally did not speak to them, respecting their need for silent meditation. However, I was once taken aback by the appearance of a monk who walked in a familiar way. As he approached me, I noticed his sharp, piercing eyes.

"I think I know you from somewhere," I said.

He looked at me and smiled. With joyful eyes and a humble expression, he said, "Do you remember the cave? I taught you how to chant."

"Lork Ta Sar! What are you doing here?" I was so excited to be with someone from Kompong Speu, the presence of whom took me back to a time when life was safe. He sat down beside me on the stone floor and began talking. It was another of those amazing occurrences at Angkor Wat that, by now, I was coming to accept.

"Where are Mr. and Mrs. Voung?" he asked.

Thinking about the Voungs always shattered any joy that had settled in my heart, but I was consoled by Lork Ta Sar's presence. It was very comforting to know that I was now with someone who had known and loved the Voungs as I had.

"We were forced to leave the cave, and they were killed by the Khmer Rouge." I cried as I told him the story of Mother Voung's capture, how I chewed through the ropes, and how Father Voung and I had escaped after watching Mother Voung die. I cried for the first time in a long time. It felt good to let the tears run down my cheeks.

"And you have been an orphan since?" he asked, sitting close to me and crying himself.

"Yes. I have had many guardians, but no family to speak of."

"Well, my chaov srey granddaughter, I came here to meet your father, Trung Chan." Trung, in the Khmer language, means prince, but I was crying too hard to understand. "He should have arrived here by now." I was shocked to learn that I had been drawn to a place where my father was headed himself. "Since he is not here, we must assume that his time has come to pass."

I began to cry again, but this time I sobbed for the father I had come so close to seeing.

"Oh, Granddaughter," Lork Ta Sar said, holding me close, "You are saarst, beautiful, like your parents, and you must remember their wish for you. They knew you were strong and humble, able to do many things. Be aware that the fighting will continue for many years, and peace will not return to Cambodia for a very long time. You will continue to suffer hardships and many more years of homelessness, but you will find peace when Cambodia finds peace."

He urged me to leave Cambodia, saying, "You must travel to another country, for your life will be threatened should you remain here." His cryptic instructions baffled me as I felt safer among the ancient ruins than I had since I left the cave. I stubbornly refused to believe him, but he was very insistent and brought the full power of his considerable personality to bear on me. In the end, I promised I would do my best to follow his advice, and in so doing, I would honor my parents.

He rose to his feet and started to leave. As he walked away, he turned and said, "You will return to Angkor Wat at the age of thirty, bringing peace with you."

After that brief visit, I never saw him in person again, although he would often appear to me in my dreams.

Not long after the visit from Lork Ta Sar, I was surprised to see Mr. Tun enter the temple courtyard. Apparently, he had questioned people in the streets around his house about whether they had seen a little girl, and someone remembered having told me the way to Angkor Wat. I knew he was back for the jewels I had stolen and then given to the servants, but as the distance between us grew smaller, I could see he did not look angry. Instead, he looked remorseful and greeted me with an apology.

"I'm sorry, Niece," he said. "I followed you here to bring you back home. You should not be on your own. It is not safe. Come with me." He stretched his hand toward me, expecting me to take it. But I would not take the hand of such a cruel and unfeeling man.

"I will not return to that house to be treated like a slave."

"Please, give me a second chance," he said.

"No, Uncle. I saw what you did to the other girls, and I hate you for it."

He grew indignant. "You want to stay here in the jungle and be eaten by a tiger? Is that what you want?"

Lork Ta Sar's words were still burning in my mind. I told him that I was resolved to go to another country and follow the path that had been laid out for me by God. I had no idea what I was saying; the words just poured forth from my lips.

"You think you know who you are, but you don't," he said, and then stunned me by beginning to speak of my parents. Lork Ta Sar had said that my father was a prince, but that was all. Mother Voung had often dropped hints about my real mother, but I was at a loss to understand how Mr. Tun could possibly know about my background. Shocked into silence, I could only listen. "I did not recognize it at first, but it soon became impossible for me to look at you without seeing your father's face," he said.

He described how he had worked with my father for the Vietnamese-backed government that had originally aided Cambodia before attempting to claim our land as their own. He also spoke of my mother's death, my father, and why we had hidden in the jungle.

"Your parents always spoke of every person's duty to take care of those who are less fortunate. That is why I am here to take you back to my house. Let Tran and I take care of you," he said.

I was surprised by his gentleness and sincerity as he spoke about my parents. His present demeanor sharply contrasted with that of his behavior toward me and the other servant girls in Phnom Penh, and I started to wonder if he was really a good man at heart who had made some terrible mistakes. Given the stressful circumstances we all lived under in Cambodia, perhaps his behavior was somewhat excusable. But I could not bear the thought of going back with him. Despite the fact that I believed he would be kind to me, I did not feel as sure that he would be kind to the other servants in the house, and I could not stand to watch them be abused. The message he carried from my parents was pure, but his actions were unacceptable. When he realized that he would be unable to convince me to leave the temple, he left the grounds, leaving behind cherished stories of my parents.

The following day, sometime in the early part of 1980, I set off walking west toward Thailand, looking for a way to get to the mysterious country for which Lork Ta Sar had said I was destined.

Thailand

The silence of the dusty roads was overwhelming. I would go for days without seeing another person, and on the occasions that I did, it was rare that we spoke. To break the silence, I sang a song to Angkor Wat:

> *Goodbye my homeland,*
> *The glorious Angkor,*
> *Glorified since the dawn.*
> *I believe I will return someday,*
> *Along with happiness, peace and prosperity.*

After a few weeks on the road from Angkor Wat, I arrived at a small village called Sisophon, about seventy miles from the Thai border. As I walked along the town's streets, I sang a new song that told of my woes as an orphan:

> *Walking through the mountain jungle,*
> *Listening to the singing cicada,*
> *I am different from the others.*
> *I am an orphan with no family,*
> *No one to shelter me.*
> *I endure hunger,*
> *And come close to death,*
> *So I raise my hands together,*
> *And beg for one full meal.*

I spotted a woman selling a tempting banana rice dessert on the side of the road. I was starving, having not found much food in recent days, and my stomach ached with a voracious hunger. I sang her my song and begged her to give me some, even though I had no money to offer in return.

"Wait, I'm busy," she said. "Can't you see I'm cleaning vegetables? If you want food, just wait."

I sat next to her in the dirt, my mouth watering as she prepared the dishes she would sell. Eventually, she set a bowl down in front of me. "Eat it all. Don't waste it," she instructed. The flavors filled my mouth and forced my lips into a smile. After I had finished every last morsel, she took me into her home.

"Thank you for saving my life," I said. She never asked me for payment, and so I believed she was a kind person with a giving heart. Her name was Theda Sarim, but I soon took to calling her Meeg, which means aunt. She had a son, Vrith, who lived with her and a husband who was working in Thailand at the time.

Despite the fact that I felt safe in her house, vibrant memories of my past filled my mind at night, and I found it difficult to sleep. So as the moon traveled across the sky, I would water the vegetable garden and stroke the side of the family cow as it slept in the barn. The plants were a vibrant shade of green, everything was fresh, and it made me feel more alive to be a part of it all. It renewed my energies, lifted my spirits, and I understood that I was truly blessed. I noticed that all the plants in the garden could be well used. The leaves could be picked and cooked for food and herbal medicines, the vegetables and fruits could be eaten, and their seeds replanted for another bountiful crop. The completeness of the garden reminded me of Angkor Wat. Whenever I sat there in the confines of the foliage, it was difficult to get up again, as my spirit was calmed by the vitality of the garden. Beautiful, waking dreams drifted through my mind and connected me to a world that I never saw while living as a recluse in the cave in Kompong Speu. Above all, it gave me hope. Night was a time for me to give and receive love from the heavens.

I would dream of touching the sunrise. The stars were bright spots shining through the clouds, foretelling the imminent rising of the sun. As I watched it ascend at dawn, I felt my soul rise with it. To this day, I hold the memory of those peaceful nights and blessed mornings where I was surrounded by the truth and compassion of nature, close to my heart. I believe that one day I will finally reach the stars and experience first hand the love and peace I see in them.

In the mornings, Aunt Theda cooked fragrant curries of chicken, coconut, sweet potatoes, and fresh herbs to sell by the roadside. It was her only form of income while her husband was away, and her diligence ensured that the house was always filled with delectable smells. While she worked, I would lead the cow to the river where people gathered to wash. I'd clean the mud and grass from her coat until it glistened. Then I'd let her graze by the riverbank while I washed myself.

I asked Aunt Theda if it would be all right for me to stay with the cow in the barn like I had on my way to Angkor Wat. "In my short life, I've spent more time living with animals than with people," I explained.

She laughed and said, "You are a silly girl," and she agreed to let me sleep in the barn. "I am thankful to have found you," she continued. "I believe you are going to change my life."

There were very few times in my life when I did not feel alone, and I cherished the time I spent with her. "You are the most unusual girl I have ever met," she once told me. Then squeezing my hand she said, "You are welcome here always, for we share a unique connection." Her passion and confidence revitalized me.

Three months after I had moved in with the Sarims, her husband, Savan, returned from the Thai border where he had been working with the United Nations to organize the refugee camps erected there to house the thousands of refugees pouring out of Cambodia. When I saw him, he looked extremely tired, and I did not want to interfere, so I hid in the back room. She cooked dinner for him and I waited, nervous that he would not accept me as readily as she had. I overheard him tell her how Chumrum Chass had been burned to the ground by the Vietnamese.

"I am very sorry for our people's loss," she said with tears in her eyes. "But, I have a surprise for you—a daughter."

He looked up, wide-eyed, as she led me out of the bedroom and into the kitchen. In his face I could see compassion and he motioned for me to sit next to him.

In 1978 the members of the Khmer Rouge Kamma-Phibal, or town governments, had arranged for the Sarim's marriage, as they had dictated every other aspect of Cambodian life. No one was free to make their own decisions about anything. To resist the authority of the Kamma-Phibal meant death, and so Savan and Theda were married. Theda was very beautiful and Savan fell in love with her quickly. For thirty-five years, he had acted as mayor in Aur Chreuv, also known as the city of Poipet. He loved serving people, and he took great pride in his country as well as in the Khmer culture, but like other pre-Khmer Rouge Cambodian officials, he hid his identity in order to avoid being executed. His compassion and sincerity are part of the reason I loved him so dearly and with all of my heart. It did not surprise him to learn that I had lost not only my parents, but many guardians as well, since the numerous years of fighting and genocide in Cambodia guaranteed that everyone had lost someone. What did surprise him was that I had escaped death so many times and had made it as far as I did.

Vrith was their only son, and I called him Bang Pros, which means older brother. We got along well together, but he was moody and unsocial a great deal of the time. He was always kind, but questioned me often about my unfailing optimism.

"Why do you always say that everything is okay? Nothing is okay. Just look around you," he would say.

"God has always taken care of us, and He will continue to do so. If we hit a rough road, we will make it through," I would say in return.

"You are nuts, little sister."

"Yes, I am," I said, and we would both smile.

I trusted them all, but was still uncomfortable sharing any significant details about myself. I knew that the truth about my heritage could get me killed, and I carefully guarded my secrets from the past. The evil ways of the Khmer Rouge and the Vietnamese made it difficult for anyone who survived their invasions to trust anybody but themselves. The way of war breeds mistrust and doubt, but they were kind and understood the dangers of telling secrets and so respected my decision. I was grateful for their understanding.

We enjoyed each other's company, and as time passed, we grew closer. We were like a real family, and eventually they asked me to tell them my name and the names of my parents. I was surprised. I had become accustomed to them simply calling me daughter or Nga. I had not expected these questions, and though I trusted them, I knew I could not give them my real name.

"Please, be honest with us," they said.

"But you see," I said, "I do not want to be forced to run for my life again."

Savan looked at his wife. "Then we would like to give you a new name, for we consider you a blessing," he said. "Would you allow us to call you Sophorn? It was the name of my daughter. She was killed by the Khmer Rouge. Will you honor us by carrying her name with you always?"

The responsibility of carrying their daughter's name weighed heavily on me, but after much thought, I gladly accepted.

"I am Sophorn," I said, and they both cried.

He said, "You are now a part of our family's blood. You are our daughter."

During the years I had spent living on the street and in the jungle, I had no real name that I could give to others. My guardians had called me by any label of their choosing, often sister or daughter, and I had grown accustomed answering to such generic names. But eventually, Sophorn became my name, and I draped myself in it like a warm cloak. When they called me Sophorn, I was wrapped in their love, for now I had a real family and a home.

Father Savan made regular trips across the mountains over the Thai border to work at the refugee camps. I knew I could not stay with the Sarims forever, and I knew that Thailand would bring me a step closer to my destiny. I asked him to take me along on his next trip. Initially, he hesitated.

"There is no way I will allow you to go there. Nothing ever happens the way we plan it to on the roads to Chumrum Trmey. It is very dangerous."

"Danger is nothing for me," I said. "Please let me go."

"Absolutely not."

"Please, Father. I beg you. I must see where the people are going." I looked deeply into his eyes, trying to make him feel what I felt.

He sighed. "You are klang and tar-su, strong and determined. I know that I cannot stop you. Even if I made you stay here with Theda, your spirit would travel with Vrith and me. Yes, you may come," he relented.

I immediately went to the barn to take leave of my friend. The cow was lying down in the warm hay, and I knelt down next to her.

"Good-bye, my friend," I said. She grunted quietly, and I sensed that she understood.

We set off that evening under a cloudless sky accompanied by Vrith. Father Savan planned to move his family to Chumrum Trmey permanently and was going to come back later for Theda after he had secured a hut for them. After walking for several hours, the air turned damp and the sky, black. Father Savan had chosen the night of the new moon for our journey so that there would be less light flooding the land. Only a tiny sliver of the moon could be seen from behind the thick, ominous clouds that had rolled in, and a blanket of ebony spread over the earth. It had rained recently, and the ground was wet and muddy. The mud sucked at our feet as we walked, pulling us into the dark muck. Decaying bodies littered the countryside as evidence of the punishment rendered upon those caught trying to escape across the border. Even though I had witnessed death many times, it was still impossible to look into their sightless eyes.

As we were passing over a wooded part of the trail, we heard the telltale sounds of soldiers ahead of us. They shone their flashlights from where they were, still somewhat far off. We dropped into the mud where we stood; Father Savan and I on opposite sides of a large tree and Vrith behind us by about three feet. The lights came closer to us, sweeping over the tall, jungle grasses, looking for refugees. But just when their lights would have lit upon us where we lay in the mud, the soldiers turned them off.

We were still in trouble, though. Without the flashlights to tell us where the soldiers were, we didn't dare move. We hid there, in the jungle, among the dead trees that had fallen across the path. I listened carefully as a soldier's footsteps came close to us. I pressed myself into the mud under a large, rotting trunk. The sound of footsteps crept closer to me still. I lay under the branches of the fallen tree as one of the Vietnamese soldiers came near me, only about six inches away. Another soldier approached him, and in so doing, placed his foot heavily upon my chest and stopped there, waiting and listening. It was so dark he could not see what it was he stepped on; he must have assumed that it was part of the underside of a fallen tree. Laying there, crushed by the weight of his monstrous boot, my nostrils invaded by the stench of rot and decay, and my ears filled with the threatening animal noises of the jungle, I felt everything and nothing all at once.

I knew that to make a sound meant certain death for all of us. I breathed shallowly and silently with my mouth closed. I was very aware of my breathing, making sure to inhale only through my nose, careful not to expand my diaphragm beneath the soldier's boot. My lungs began to ache. Not being able to take full, deep breaths, made me feel as if I were drowning. But life had taught me that the only way to survive the enemy was to be patient and determined. No matter how much pain they caused me, I would not reveal myself through weakness. The pain was incredibly intense, and I kept praying that they would go away. I wanted to get out from the mud, out into open space, to fill my lungs with fresh air. But they stood there, looking and listening. After what seemed like hours, the patrol passed on without seeing us. I took a deep breath and filled my lungs.

Father Savan and Vrith crawled over to where I lay, unmoving with cold and panic. "Sophorn, my daughter, are you all right?" he whispered, wiping the mud from my face with his own muddy hand.

I tried to sit up, but the pain was so extreme that I could not move my arms or upper body. "My chest hurts, Father. The soldier stood on me," I said.

He grabbed me and held me in his strong arms, cradling me close. I could feel his heart beating through his torso. He kept telling me that everything was going to be all right, but I knew he was attempting to convince himself of this just as much as me.

"Do not cry," he said. But it hurt more than I could bear. The intake of each breath caused my chest to burn at the spot where the soldier's foot had bruised it.

We waited until the patrol was a safe distance away before we continued our journey, and we finally crossed the border just before daylight. By late morning, we arrived in Chumrum Chass, now only the charred remains of a village. It had been burned and the people had been killed or run off. Father Savan cried at the blackened reminder of what a difficult battle it was that we were fighting. As soon as a camp was set up, the Vietnamese army would destroy it in their ongoing effort to keep Cambodian refugees out of Thailand. Officially, it had been known as Site One, with Site Two being Chumrum Trmey, a little bit further from the border. We began walking toward Chumrum Trmey.

Amazingly, the camp was alive and thriving when we arrived. Plentiful housing consisted of a combination of military tents, makeshift dwellings formed by blue tarpaulins slung over poles and huts augmented with palm leaves. It was the dry season and the weather was so hot that it felt like the entire world might burst into flames at any moment. Space was limited, so we were forced to camp near a huge termite nest made of red earth.

We stayed at Chumrum Trmey for three months while Father Savan did business with the Thai villagers in surrounding areas, earning money to return home. One day, Vrith and I dug a pit in which to build a fire for cooking our lunch. We were dirty and tired, but our hunger needed to be satisfied before we could wash or sleep. Vrith continued to add small sticks and dried leaves until the fire was a decent size. The bigger the fire, the faster we could cook the small bits of meat we had received from the other refugees.

Something flew over our heads, but I didn't know what. It was quiet and flew by with a woosh, so I assumed it was a bird. Vrith saw it, too, and looked at me over the fire. Then there were a series of pops, probably caused by children playing with twigs nearby.

"How can kids play those games right now? Don't they know it's not a time to have fun?" Vrith said, obviously irritated.

A scream ripped through the air, and that's when everyone began to run. The pops began again, this time unceasingly, and for every pop a refugee fell down dead. The camp had been suddenly and violently attacked by the Vietnamese. The soldiers spoke clearly and loudly, directing everyone to run if they wanted to live. "Di, Di!" they yelled, which in Vietnamese means go.

Where will we run to? No matter where we go, we can't escape, I thought.

Rapidly, a familiar scene developed before me. Refugees were running wildly, frantically seeking a safe place to hide. But while they ran, I didn't. I was tired of running.

"If we die, we die here," I said to Vrith. We stayed in front of the fire pit and tried to cook, unwilling to acknowledge the onset of violence. I ignored the commotion until I couldn't any longer.

My resolve turned to panic when I saw a gun pointed in my direction. For the seventh time in my life, I found myself in the midst of murderers. The camp was as I imagined hell to be, full of blood and screams.

Vrith picked me up and threw me away from the fire pit seconds before it was hit by mortar fire. I covered my head and neck, my muscles tensed and ready for the bullet that would inevitably strike me. The firing in my immediate area ceased, and I looked up. Vrith was nowhere to be seen.

The soldiers came from every direction. They stood on the top of a nearby hill randomly shooting down at the innocent civilians. The raging sounds of machine guns deafened us as their bullets fell like a rain upon the common people.

I ran toward the nearest trench seeking protection. I tried to crouch beside the six people who had already taken refuge in it, but as quickly as I jumped in, they pushed me out.

"There is no room. Get out!" they screamed.

Scrambling to my feet above the trench, I tried hard to keep focused on survival. A grenade landed at my feet, but miraculously failed to explode. I ran, and a moment later a second grenade exploded in the trench where I had tried to hide. My life was saved by those who pushed me from the trench in an effort to save their own. People ran, tripping over each other as they blindly tried to escape death and the destruction of their safe haven. Young or old, it did not matter—we all ran.

One woman called for help from underneath a pile of debris where she lay buried. I ran to her and grabbed her hand. She looked up at me, her eyes smiling with courage.

"Let me pull you up," I said. I never looked back at the dead bodies in the trench, but I wished that I could have saved them all. However, this woman here was alive, the only one I could possibly help. I pulled, but her body would not move. An immense sadness swept over me as I realized that I would not be able to save her. I was helpless against the enemy and surrounded by the dead.

The world collapsed in front of me. Many unanswerable questions invaded my mind as I struggled to understand why this was happening again. What motivated the Vietnamese to kill so many innocent Cambodians? When would I find the peace that Lork Ta Sar had spoken of? I began to feel numb, my adrenaline keeping me anesthetized to the tragedy surrounding me. This new war was merely a repetition of the previous ones. And like it had in the others, the sounds of fighting eventually faded into the distance, but only after many innocent lives had been violently ended.

Silence enveloped the camp. The deceased rested on the ground, their mortal wounds exposed. I remember feeling a bullet fly right over the top of my head, and I watched as it fell to the ground in front of me. Yet the people who had been running next to me weren't so lucky. It was not fair to those people or their families, and I wished that the bullets would have taken my life instead.

I called for Father Savan, hoping he had returned from the outlying villages and had survived the attack. I called for him until my throat became sore and raw, but I could not find him or Vrith anywhere. I prayed that they were safe, that death had not found them. Orphaned children, separated from their loved ones, surrounded me. They huddled close, crying and screaming. I tried to avoid thinking the worst, but the thought kept fighting its way into my mind—I was once again one of them. Although I had known Father Savan for only a short time, I loved him as dearly as I loved my real father. The thought that I might lose him forever left me devastated.

CHAPTER TEN

Khao I Dang

I soon found myself on the road with hundreds of other camp inhabitants trying to escape the bombardment, trying to outrun the violence. We kept moving away from the camp; no one wanted to stay near a place that that reeked of terror. I followed the crowd, not knowing what else to do and having nowhere else to go. I certainly did not want to return to the camp alone, and returning to Aunt Theda in Sisophon was impossible at this point. Despite the fact that she seemed to be the only family I had left, I had to keep moving toward my destiny.

By now, I had become accustomed to this constant trekking from one place to another and I had forgotten what it felt like to have a home. I tried not to think about the cave in Kompong Speu and instead tried to make wherever it was I slept feel like home. But no matter how hard I tried to love the ditch I was sleeping in, it never felt that way.

I survived on the small amounts of food I was able to beg from the other refugees. I do not know how long I traveled like this, but eventually I ended up in the Phnom Chat Mountains of Cambodia, close to the Laotian border. I felt the inexplicable need to travel alone, to head in my own direction, even though I didn't know what direction that was. So after many miles I drifted off from the main group of refugees and was traveling more or less alone. I liked being on my own, but it was a comfort to know that my solitude was merely physical, for God traveled with me within my heart. I walked until the day I was picked up by a Khmer Rouge patrol and taken to a training camp for child soldiers in the Phnom Chat Mountains.

When asked my age, I lied and told the soldiers that I was only five years old to avoid being forced into combat. All sides in the conflict were training young children to be soldiers. At ten or twelve years of age, a child knew how to operate a gun, and at fifteen they were recruited into the army.

Our life in the camp was similar to the Hanoi camp I had previously escaped from—very austere and strictly disciplined. We were subjected to political propaganda talks and exhausting military exercises, marching up and down the parade grounds they had cleared in the jungle. As usual, there was little food and water, and we stayed in rudimentary huts built on the side of the mountain. Despite the freezing temperatures at night, each of us was only given a single blanket to sleep under. Many children succumbed to the harsh conditions and died before ever having a chance to live.

I was hungry, cold, and miserable, so as soon as I had the chance, I left. I simply started walking away from the camp, determined to keep walking no matter who tried to stop me, but amazingly no one tried. It was as if there was an invisible shield around me, and I was able to pass over the camp borders unseen. *Thank you, God, for protecting me. Please, protect the other children as well,* I thought.

I left with the realization that children are the most vulnerable in a war. Their young minds, which are eager to learn, are easily led astray by those who would use them to do harm to others. The Khmer Rouge were passionate about their way of life and determined to achieve their goal of controlling Cambodia. Had they used their resources for the promotion of good and not evil, the children of the training camp may have grown up with hearts of love, not hatred. Many children left that camp, indoctrinated by the Khmer Rouge and hating anyone who was against it. I am so very lucky that I was able to leave before my heart, too, had hardened.

I tried to retrace the path that had taken me to this camp, hoping to make it out of the mountains and back to Chumrum Trmey. I hoped Father Savan and Vrith had survived the raid, returned to Sisophon for Aunt Theda, and relocated to a safer part of Thailand as planned. I was optimistic that I would be able to locate them through the refugee camp. Getting there would be another grueling journey—another hundred miles on foot—but I was motivated by the hope of finding my family. But when I finally reached Chumrum Trmey, the Sarims were not there, and no one at the camp knew anything of their whereabouts. Devastated, I felt the extreme loss of family yet again.

It had only been a month or so since Chumrum Trmey had been so violently annihilated and relief workers were still in the area, helping any survivors or new arrivals who had not heard of the camp's closure, to relocate. As soon as I arrived, a French relief doctor took me under his wing. His fair complexion was a striking contrast to the darker skin of us Cambodians. He was tall and incredibly handsome, but most importantly, he was kind and funny. He made me laugh at a time when laughter was rarely heard. He encouraged me to leave Cambodia.

"You should go to France," he said. "Many refugees are immigrating there."

"No, Doctor, I can't," I said. Despite how much safer it would be in France, my heart told me that this was not where I was supposed to go, and that this was not what Lork Ta Sar had meant for me.

"Then go to the Redlands. From there, you may be able to go to America," he said. At the mention of America, I felt a thrill shoot through my spine. I hardly knew anything about the somewhat mythical country, but I could already feel the freedom of America inside of me.

Thousands of refugees were on the move through the hot, oppressive weather toward the Redlands. We were attacked by anti-refugee squads often, rocket and rifle fire forcing us to scuttle and dive into the ditches for safety. Many people were injured, and we left them to die on the side of the road because there was no one to tend to them. We had become numb to the continued killing. When eyes see so much mindless slaughter day after day, the mind switches off and the eyes do not see anymore. But there was one incident I could not ignore. I was offered the warm blood of a recently slaughtered cow to drink. I was starving, so I attempted to swallow some, but I could not drink it. I remembered how kind the cow had been to me on the way to Angkor Wat and the gentleness of the Sarim's cow. Despite my raging hunger, the blood gagged in my throat and I had to spit it out.

It must have been late in 1980 when I arrived at the Redlands. Named for the rusty color of the volcanic rock that forms its landscape, it was a barren and dusty land. No one wanted to stay there for very long, but once there, we were informed by relief workers that only families, not individuals, were being permitted to leave. In order to escape my war-torn homeland, I would need to find myself a new family—not an easy task in a society that was suddenly plagued by orphans.

Busses left daily for Khao I Dang, the transit camp from which you could immigrate to America, each of them filled with hopeful refugees. I wandered around the makeshift dwellings of cardboard remnants and bits of canvas that had been erected in the camp, keeping an eye out for any potential families to travel with. I came across a family I vaguely recognized from my stay in Chumrum Trmey and climbed on board a bus with them. The mother of the family was a petite woman who wore bright, polka dot-patterned tank tops over her sarong. Her husband had been a member of the Cambodian army but had passed away, and she was left to look after their nine children alone. I can still remember the scent of baby powder she used on her face in place of makeup and the smell of the toasted coconut oil she combed into her short, shiny hair. Her name was Mrs. Touch.

She refused to let me stay with them on the bus at first, insisting that I go find someone else instead.

"But Om Srey, I need to go with you," I said.

She shook her head. "I already have nine children. I don't need another one."

I ignored her protests and stayed on board. The bus was really a truck with a canvas roof and no seats. Everyone stood for the drive, packed together tightly, like sardines in a cheap tin can. It was incredibly hot and the air stunk of body odor. Our destination, Khao I Dang, was run by the Thai government, despite the fact that it was on the Cambodian side of the border. It was one of several large camps that processed immigrants to the United States and several other countries. We heard that Rosalynn Carter, the wife of President Jimmy Carter, had paid a much publicized visit there in November of 1979. It was a special time for the refugees and a memorable one. She was the first person of international importance to recognize our plight and for her to actually come to see us meant a great deal to the people. It buoyed our hearts immensely. To this day, everyone in the Cambodian community remembers Mrs. Carter with deep affection for the kindness and generosity of spirit she brought to us. We will always consider her as one of our dearest allies.

By the time we reached Khao I Dang, Mrs. Touch had relented and allowed me to stay with her. I thought she did so out of the kindness of her heart, but I would later feel differently. I was excited to be in a new place with a new family. We were taking positive steps forward, steps that led to America where a life free from the constant presence of war awaited us.

The camp was staffed by U.N. relief workers and policed by Thai soldiers. We were housed in bamboo-framed huts with roofs fashioned out of palm leaves. The floors were raised slightly off the ground and the beds were set on platforms. Young girls of the camp would often hide under these platforms at night to avoid the attention of Thai soldiers who went prowling through the camp for sex. The toilets were buckets, hidden from view by curtains that hung from bamboo poles. Although the curtains hid these rudimentary toilets from view, they could not hide the awful smell of human excrement. The conditions of our temporary home were extremely unsanitary and revolting.

We used empty juice bottles and other plastic containers that had been discarded by the soldiers and U.N. workers to carry the water for drinking and washing that came to us by truck. The water was often tainted, but the only way to know whether it was clean or not was to wait and see if anyone got sick from drinking it. To get enough water for the eleven of us in the Touch family, I had to make several trips a day and stand in line for hours. If I arrived too late in the morning, the water would be gone. Despite this, we had most of the basic necessities of life, and compared to the places we had been before, it was relatively safe. The aid workers gave us blankets, clothes, and food rations. Some children went to a makeshift school that had been erected within the confines of the camp, and there was a day care center and even a small hospital. When I had free time, I liked to sit outside the window of the school and listen to the lessons. It was there that I learned my first English word, beauty.

There were also small luxuries that we sometimes indulged in. There was a thriving market in monosodium glutamate, a popular salty seasoning that made our bland food taste like the finest delicacy. Sometimes, we would sneak out of the camp and head to the villages near the border to find firewood and sugar, two things that were always in short supply. But the most cherished luxury at the camp was its relative safety. The children could play together without worry, and even the adults were able to enjoy some recreation, such as boxing matches against the Thai soldiers. At Khao I Dang, we all took a little time to enjoy being alive. This was a kind of comfort I did not experience much in my childhood.

Although I longed to play with the other children, I did not have much time for silliness and games. I had to work to earn my keep with the Touch family. At first, Mrs. Touch was reasonably nice to me, but she soon made it clear that I was not equal to her own children, and that she considered me their servant. I let them call me Nga, the affectionate nickname bestowed upon me by Chandra Sam before he died, but I never felt any affection from them. In fact, life with the Touches was quite the opposite. Most of her children were pitiless and cruel, but I did have something of a friend in Bang Soka, one of Mrs. Touch's oldest daughters. Like the others, she could sometimes be unkind, but I felt an inexplicable closeness to her.

I never complained about the abuse I suffered at their hands for I knew that if I reported the abuse to anyone, we would lose our chance to go to America. I understood that survival meant enduring seemingly unbearable hardships, and with America as my goal, I would do whatever it took to get there.

To supplement her income, Mrs. Touch sold fish paste, cupcakes, beans, and banana desserts, or rather, I did. Every day, after waking early to prepare these items, I was sent out to sell them along the streets of the camp. I carried the food in a flat bamboo basket on my head as I walked around the block. Though I did all the work, Mrs. Touch kept a close eye on the profits. When I did not bring home the right amount, she or one of her sons would beat me as a punishment. Occasionally, it would rain and ruin everything or the food would be stolen while I daydreamed about life in America, and when the food was lost, Mrs. Touch punished me severely.

A rumor circulated among the refugees that a fortune teller had predicted a Koun Khmeng Nack Meanbun, a Child of the Spirit, would arrive at Khao I Dang bringing international justice to Cambodia. Some people of the camp trusted in the prophecies of fortune tellers, but I thought little of their predictions.

The day after I heard the rumor, I was out selling food and enjoying the freedom of having the day to myself. I meandered along the street and observed my surroundings, experiencing life in Khao I Dang.

After finding a place in the middle of the street, I sat down and began to advertise my fare. I noticed a Thai soldier watching me from a distance, and I assumed that he was considering making a purchase. I did my best to entice him. "My food is crunchy, hot, and good!" I yelled. "It's tasty and delicious!"

He approached and looked at me sternly. "What is your name?" he asked.

"Nga," I said. "Would you like to buy something to eat?" I gestured toward my basket of beans and cakes.

"I don't want your food. You must come to the police station with me." And with that he grabbed my arm, pulling me up from where I sat. My basket fell to the ground, spilling my food into the dirt.

Struggling to get free from his grasp, I asked, "What do you want? I didn't do anything wrong!"

I broke free and he chased after me, yelling, "Koun Khmeng Nack Meanbun!" I ran as fast as I could, praying to God for help. Suddenly, a woman appeared in the doorway of a nearby hut. She heard the soldier calling me Child of the Spirit and pulled me into her home. Amazingly, the soldier did not see where I had gone, and I was safe.

I never learned the name of the woman who saved me, and after she walked me home, I never saw her again. I did not relate the incident to Mrs. Touch out of fear that she wouldn't believe me, even though I knew I would be beaten for the missing profits from that day's sales.

Despite our relief at being safe from the war, we did not feel completely protected in the camp. The Thai soldiers who guarded the camp were often brutal, stealing from us and raping the women. They attacked two teenage girls in their hut; they beat and raped them repeatedly before dumping their pummeled bodies in the brush. I was near when they were found, and so I helped to carry the girls to the clinic for treatment. Blood covered their bodies and stained their ripped clothing. One of the girls was unable to walk or talk and I felt great pity for both of them.

During this time, young children began to disappear from Khao I Dang. It was believed that they were being kidnapped by the Thai soldiers and sold into prostitution in Bangkok, Japan, Vietnam, and other countries. Now that I knew that some of the soldiers and refugees of the camp believed me to be the Khmeng Nack Meanbun, I felt especially vulnerable. A number of children, including myself, were determined to protect ourselves and our friends. We appealed to a relief worker, a woman we simply called "the gray-haired lady," for help. She was genuinely concerned about what we said and helped us to petition the U.N. authorities for help. It was dangerous for us to speak against the soldiers. They had immense power over our lives and always sought retribution for those who caused them trouble. But we were brave children and told our stories to anyone who would listen. It was one of my first experiences with social activism, and it did not go unrewarded; the United Nations heard us and began to take action to restrain the soldiers. The other refugees were proud of us and the measures we had taken to protect ourselves and our people.

When Mrs. Touch heard about my role in this, she became infuriated, afraid there would be recrimination against her family by the soldiers. She slapped me and beat me while her son pounded me with a large bamboo stick. Like the ones that came before, I endured this beating as I did the many that followed. I needed to be part of a family to get to America, and Mrs. Touch was my only hope.

Our first two applications for immigration to the United States were rejected because Mrs. Touch claimed that I was her real daughter. The differences in our facial features and skin color made it easy to see that this was not the case. The members of the Touch family had much darker skin than mine, and because of my Japanese heritage, I carried sharper facial features than most Cambodians. All we could do was apply for immigration a third time and hope for a better result.

My treatment by the Touches seemed to improve after a fortune-teller told Mrs. Touch that I was a special child with the blessings of Buddha, and that I would bring them much happiness if they treated me with kindness. I did not concern myself with the possibility of having any "special blessings," but they hit me less after that, and I was relieved to have a respite from the beatings.

At some point, our family was moved to another camp, this one called Chumrum Chhunbury, where we applied for immigration again. This time, Mrs. Touch admitted I was adopted and the application was approved. On November 13, 1983, at the age of eleven, after eight years of living on the run or in refugee, military and prison camps, without family and with little food, I finally boarded a bus bound for the airport at Bangkok. I was going to the country we Cambodians called Amayreekaing.

CHAPTER ELEVEN

Houston

I had never traveled on a plane before and just to see one of these enormous machines up close was absolutely incredible. The only planes I had seen before were the ones that had dropped bombs on our homes. But this was a commercial plane, built for comfort, not killing. The piercing whine of the engines as they started to turn thrilled me. As the plane lurched forward and slowly gained speed, I felt my heart rate increase. The strange feeling of gravity pulling me into the seat as the wheels left the ground was unlike anything I had ever experienced. *This is the start of a new life,* I thought.

I sat at a window seat and gazed out the window while the others slept. I tried to memorize the beauty of the sky by closing my eyes and picturing it in my mind. The sky had many layers, each one of them more beautiful than the next. The billowy white clouds resting upon the baby blue of the sky was all topped with the crystal clarity of what must have been the gates to heaven. I was not afraid.

My moment of peace was broken when the snore of Bang Soka ripped through the silence of the sleeping plane. I tried to shut the noise out, to regain that serenity I had so briefly felt, but it was impossible. Her nasal groaning was too much to bear.

"Wake up," I said. "You're snoring." I nudged her in the arm a little.

"What?" she asked, rubbing her eyes.

"It's the worst sound in the world."

She laughed, closed her eyes, and fell back asleep. I turned back to the window.

Our first stop on what was to be an 8,000 mile trip was Hong Kong. The tall buildings and bright neon signs were amazing to behold, as our eyes were more accustomed to the darkness of a deep jungle than the sparkling brightness of a major city. As we were driven from the airport to the hotel, we passed by department stores filled with goods so luxurious that we could have never even imagined they existed before that day. We pressed our faces to the windows of the bus in amazement. Had I known about Disneyland, I would have believed we were there, so extensive was my joy and awe. From our hotel room, which along with our flight had been arranged and paid for by the United States YMCA, I could see people practicing Tai Chi in a nearby park early the next morning. Their body movements were slow and peaceful. It made me wonder how Cambodia could be so different, so violent, and so miserable.

That evening we had a huge feast with roast duck, pork, and many types of desserts. We were in heaven. Although we loved the native dishes of our homeland, we had never tasted food such as this. It was a new spectrum of flavors and smells in quantities that were hard to fathom. I was tempted to fill my pockets with the leftovers in case I never had the chance to eat like this again. It was a moment of sublime happiness. We went to bed that night stuffed to the point of bursting, reveling in the clean, cotton sheets, soft carpets, hot showers, and real flushing toilets of our room.

The next morning we left for San Francisco en route to Houston, Texas, our final destination. I was now certain that America was the world that Lork Ta Sar had spoken of. Everything about this trip felt incredibly right, and I prayed that I was doing what God had intended me to do. It was a long flight to San Francisco, and I do not remember much of it, except that eventually the excitement of being on a plane faded, and I grew tired of being in such a confined space. I had lived most of my life outdoors and spending all these hours in a metal and plastic tube felt unnatural. I couldn't wait to be back on land, out in the open air.

In San Francisco the weather was cold, and we were given warm parkas to wear by the people from the YMCA who met us at the airport and helped us change flights. My parka was pink with green stripes and the first piece of new clothing I had ever owned. I slipped it on, zipped it up, and shoved my hands in the pockets. Wrapped in its warmth, I was ready to face whatever America had to offer.

Six hours and an additional plane ride later, we arrived in Texas. It was winter and the weather was cooler, so my new coat was useful and appreciated. A man from the YMCA, who we were told to call Mr. Jim, met us at the airport. He was six feet tall, substantially taller than us, and he smiled a lot. He told us not to worry and assured us that we were finally safe—I wish he had been right. I allowed myself to become caught up in the excitement of being in America and could not have imagined that more difficulties were to come into my life.

For the moment, however, there were many things to do before we could become settled. First, there were the medical examinations. A series of doctors poked and prodded us and gave us injections. Everything in the clinic seemed so shiny, clean, and bright, including the people who worked there. The doctors and nurses were extremely kind, and it was so different from anything we had known before. After we were given medical clearance, Mr. Jim took us to a Goodwill thrift store to buy clothes. They allowed each of us to choose five new outfits. Five outfits! We were so thrilled by the wealth and generosity to which we were being exposed. These were the first real clothes I had owned since leaving the cave eight years earlier—never again would I have to wear garments made of leaves or the dreaded Khmer Rouge uniform. Clothed in a T-shirt and jeans, I felt like an American angel.

We spent those first few weeks in a house owned by the YMCA. It was very large, and we shared it with ten other immigrant families from Vietnam, South Africa, Laos, and Cambodia as well as a few YMCA staff members. I do not remember what part of the city it was in; Houston seemed so vast when compared to the confinement of the refugee camps where we had spent the past three years. Our first night there, we were kept awake until the early morning hours by the excitement of being in such a new and different place. Consequently, we slept late into the next morning. Unaware that we had slept halfway through Thanksgiving Day, we were completely surprised to find the YMCA workers in the kitchen, putting the finishing touches on an enormous feast. There were giant stuffed turkeys surrounded by special arrangements of colorful vegetables. Overflowing bowls of mashed potatoes, gravy, cranberries, and biscuits made our mouths water. All I could think was *Am I dreaming?* The YMCA workers smiled at the astonishment that showed on our faces.

Unsure that this food was for us, we were reluctant to approach the table. We stood there, gazing at what was before us with happy smiles on our faces, breathing in the intoxicating aromas. One of the workers spoke Khmer and told us that the food was there for us to enjoy. We stole glances at each other that said, *Is this for real?*

We gathered around the table and gave thanks to God for providing us with this new chance at life. Our prayer of gratitude carried with it the very essence of the Thanksgiving holiday. The first Pilgrims, refugees like ourselves, had seen for the first time in this feast a glimmer of hope and an assurance of our future. We expressed our appreciation to the YMCA and thanked everyone who was taking care of us. This was the first American food we had ever tasted, and we ate until we could eat no more.

Everything calmed down after Thanksgiving Day, and it was a few short weeks later when we were introduced to Christmas. Homes in the neighborhood became the backdrop of a hundred fantastically designed light shows. We wondered what kind of place this Houston was, for through the front window of every home, a large tree with blinking lights could be seen. We quickly learned to accept the American holiday as joyfully as you can imagine one would after having been constantly on the run for so many years. With the arrival of Christmas Day came our own decorated tree with many beautiful boxes beneath its boughs. The workers began to exchange gifts with one another, and then when gift after gift was presented to us, we felt spoiled and embarrassed. After having had so much taken away from us, it was the first time in our lives that we had been given things in abundance. It was a time of many firsts, including my first visit to a Christian church. I found Christian beliefs to be very compelling and I immediately opened my heart with the faith that Jesus would enter.

New Year's Day was just as memorable, and we all felt that if the rest of our time in this new land was going to be anything like the first two months, then we were truly in a magical place. Shortly after January 1, 1984, we moved into an apartment building and began to collect food stamps from the government. Mrs. Touch used them to buy all sorts of American foods such as macaroni and cheese, hot dogs, and cereal. I went to school for the first time along with the other children in the Touch family. Being inside a classroom was very different from sitting outside of one, and I was embarrassed because I could not read or write my own name. My English amounted to the few words I had picked up listening through the window at the school in the refugee camp. I struggled with the lessons at first, but with the help of some of the other kids in my ESL class, I began to master basic English.

Despite my young age, I was allowed to help out around the YMCA and earn a little money. Once I had saved five dollars, I put the money in an envelope and saved it until the temptation to spend it was too great. After school one day, I walked to the neighborhood grocery store to buy some food and something to drink. I was very hungry, but I was overwhelmed by all the food choices on the shelves. I could not read the words so I tried to determine what was inside each package by looking at the pictures. I picked out a package with a handsome cartoon dog on the bag that reminded me of the tiger on the box of Frosted Flakes Mrs. Touch once brought home. After shaking the box a few times I purchased it, believing it was filled with cookies, cereal, or some sort of candy. I left the store, tore open the bag, and ate some.

This tastes yummy, I said to myself. The cookies were salty and crunchy and altogether very satisfying. The next day, I took the box to my classmates and teacher at school. I wanted to show them what I had accomplished on my own. I felt self-sufficient and was proud of myself.

But when I showed them the box, they pointed at me and laughed.

"What's wrong?" I asked, not understanding what the joke was.

"You ate dog biscuits!" they said.

I felt angry, confused, and hurt. When I lived in the refugee camp, I had to pick up food from the street if I wanted to live. I used to wait for people to throw their plates away so that I could eat whatever bits they left. This was the only way I could survive. My classmates had no concept of the extent of human suffering to which some people had experienced.

"Do you think you could survive in the jungles of Cambodia? With no food and nothing to drink, you would be grateful to have these to eat," and I shook the box of biscuits. "What would you do if someone threw you in an interrogation box and tortured you, or you were left alone in the middle of a gunfight?"

My outburst stunned them all, and they said nothing. I realized that I had been harsh with my words, and I tried to make amends.

"I'm just like you, but at the same time, I am very different. Please tell me why this is not okay to eat."

"That's easy," one of them said. "People food tastes good. Dog food tastes like poo."

"You're crazy," I exclaimed. "These taste just like regular cookies! Here, try it and see."

They giggled, refusing to taste it. No one seemed upset or angry with me for my outburst, and although I was embarrassed by my mistake, I was glad to finally be able to laugh, even if it was at myself.

The friendliness I found in my new schoolmates was in sharp contrast to the treatment I received at home. Bang Soka had married and moved out of our apartment not long after we arrived in Houston, and when she left, I felt as if I had lost a sister. Once in America, Mrs. Touch seemed to forget the words of the fortune-teller and my frequent beatings resumed. After school each day, she sent me out to gather empty soda cans that she would then recycle at the local grocery store. On days that I did not bring home enough cans, I would not be allowed to eat. She made quite a few dollars from the cans I collected and was soon able to purchase a used sewing machine from a pawn shop around the corner. I no longer had to collect cans, as I was then put to work sewing clothes. I worked until midnight every night after school, sewing dresses and pants, which she then sold at the local swap meet. I had no time for homework and regularly fell asleep in class sprawled across my desk. The teachers were very understanding. They knew I was dealing with many changes and trying to adapt to this new culture. They tried to help, but my grades still suffered. Not surprisingly, my poor academic performance never seemed to be of much concern to Mrs. Touch.

A friend of Mrs. Touch had moved to California before we did and sent word that there was a large Cambodian population living there. Mrs. Touch wanted to be near her own people, so in 1985, she decided to move our family from Texas to California, even though we had only started to feel comfortable there. We did not relish the thought of moving yet again, but we did not have a choice, as this is what Mrs. Touch wanted. Her friend drove from Long Beach to pick us up, and we left our apartment home in Houston, cramming ourselves into the woman's old van. We drove for hours down desert roads, not knowing much about our final destination, only that it would be filled with people like us. It was cold outside, but the interior of the van was warm with people. It was very cramped and uncomfortable, and reminded me of our flight to America. That night, I was too anxious to sleep, but Mrs. Touch's children had no problem and they snored loudly. The noise, the heat, and my innate need to be cautious and alert while traveling was enough to give me a horrible headache. I stared out the windows into the desert night in anticipation of seeing our new home.

In the middle of the night we arrived at the corner of Anaheim Street and Dawson Avenue. I immediately felt that we did not belong, that we should be back in Houston. The streets were dark and dirty and suspicious people wandered the alleys. I believed that it was a bad idea for us to move here, but Mrs. Touch thought that it was for the best. We stayed in a tiny apartment on Dawson Avenue along with two other Cambodian families. There were only two rooms for sixteen people to share. To say the apartment was far too crowded is an understatement. Every morning, we waited in line for our turn to use the bathroom and cooked and ate in shifts. The cramped conditions bred fighting and our apartment was never quiet. It was a very difficult and depressing way to live.

Mrs. Touch kept me working late every night sewing clothes, and during the day I struggled to stay awake in class at Hill Jr. High School, where I had enrolled. Life was the same as it had been in Texas—I never had enough time to do my homework, my grades dropped, I was constantly tired, and I was regularly beaten for not being productive enough. But I did my best to stay positive, consistently praying for better conditions. Unfortunately things only got worst.

I was so exhausted by the late nights and continual beatings at home that I became seriously depressed. I had escaped one kind of torment in Cambodia only to end up in a new kind of American hell. Bang Soka was still living in Houston with her husband, and I had no one to confide in. In my desperate, thirteen-year-old state of mind, I tried to end my life. All I knew was that I couldn't go on living with the way things were.

I grabbed all the pills I could find in the bathroom medicine cabinet at home and took them to school with me. I asked to be excused from my class on a hall pass, and I went to the restroom and started swallowing as many of them as I could. Fortunately, only a small amount of aspirin and painkillers made it into my system before a teacher walked in and saw what I was attempting to do. I was taken to the emergency room at a local hospital for treatment where I was asked repeatedly why I had tried to commit suicide, but I kept silent. From my experience in Cambodia, I had learned to not reveal anything while under interrogation. I knew that what I revealed could be used against me.

Since I refused to speak, I was sent to the Chestnut Mental Clinic in Long Beach where I was put on antidepressants. I knew there was no way I could explain my life at home without having to face the wrath of Mrs. Touch. I never swallowed the tablets they gave me, but kept them under my tongue and spat them down the toilet as soon as the nurse left the room. No one noticed this and after being under observation for a week, I returned home, back to the place that was the primary source of my unhappiness.

Long Beach

The next few years of my life passed by in a haze of depression, lone-liness, and despair. There were very few moments of relief from the intense and oppressive sadness in my head and heart. I lived as if confined to an inescapable cage. Moving in a kind of mental fog that clouded my vision and dulled my senses, I worked, ate, slept, and went to school—and I did all of it completely alone. Despite the fact that I was in an apartment crowded with people, I had never felt lonelier, and my heart had never felt so empty. I was not living life; I was still just trying to survive it.

We moved from the apartment on Dawson to one three miles away on Pacific Avenue. My depression worsened, and I made another failed attempt at taking my own life by once again swallowing an excessive amount of pills. This led to another spell at Chestnut, after which, Mrs. Touch decided that the best way to cure my depression and simultane-ously get rid of me would be to marry me off as quickly as possible. I was only fourteen years old and not of legal age to be married in the United States, but she was accustomed to the Cambodian tradition of arranging marriages for children at a very young age.

It wasn't long before she introduced me to her groom of choice, one of the social workers who paid us monthly visits to make sure we had enough food stamps and were not living in complete squalor. He seemed extremely old, feeble, and disgusting to me, and I absolutely refused to have anything to do with him.

"He's handsome. Many girls would be pleased to have such a distinguished man for a husband," she said.

"If you think he's so handsome, you should marry him yourself!" I said. I may have been depressed, but my tongue was still sharp.

Inflamed by my impudence, Mrs. Touch exploded. She slapped me hard across the cheek and started beating me with her fists. "Get out!" she shouted. "Leave and never return!"

I did not fight her, as I had no reason to fight. It was my chance to go.

The apartment was on an upper level, above a garage. The garage had space for four cars but was usually half-empty, so I grabbed a few clothes and my backpack full of schoolbooks and moved into my new home downstairs.

Southern California has a temperate climate, but in the winter months the nights can get very cold. I had no pillows or blankets to keep me warm, only a thin jacket. I slept huddled in a ball on the bare concrete floor between two cars that belonged to our neighbors. By rising early and staying out late, I was able to live there without being noticed. In the mornings, I washed my face in cold water from a utility faucet in the corner, but I still went to school smelling foul. I tried to keep myself clean, but a single faucet is no substitute for a shower and soap, and my classmates began to comment on my body odor. I bathed under the faucet every night and tried to scrub away the smell, but the cold water stung my skin, and I nearly froze to death.

I was humiliated and ashamed because I only had a few outfits to change into and these I could only wash in the sink, without detergent. Often my only meal was the free lunch I was given at school every day. I worked a few odd jobs after school to earn some money and avoided making contact with the Touch family upstairs. As a minor, I was still legally bound to Mrs. Touch, but there was no way I was going to live with her. She seemed glad to be rid of me and acted as if I did not exist. I sat down every night and tried to determine what I could have done to bring this upon myself. I asked God why he continued to punish me, but

I never got an answer.

After one too many miserable nights on that hard concrete floor, I realized that I could not continue living as I had been. Late one Friday evening during the Christmas season of 1985, after spending a few months in the garage and unwilling to face one more night of bone-aching sleep on the cold floor, I grabbed my few possessions, walked out onto the street, and hopped on a bus headed downtown. It was close to midnight when I arrived in the center of Long Beach, and the streets were deserted except for a few late-night revelers. My plan started and ended with the bus ride downtown, and I had no idea what to do next, so I set off walking down Pacific Coast Highway from the corner of Long Beach Boulevard, heading north toward Los Angeles. As a homeless refugee in Cambodia, I was used to letting my feet take me wherever they wanted, and I would wander off in whatever direction seemed right at the time. That night my old habits kicked in, and I headed north up PCH.

City streets at night have their own rules of survival, and I tried to remain as alert as I had been while traveling through the Cambodian jungles. Unfortunately, as I walked along the dark road past the shuttered storefronts, my mind, like my feet, began to wander, and I lost awareness of my surroundings. I was shaken from my lonely introspection by the screeching of brakes and loud, booming music coming from a long, dark car that jerked to a stop alongside of me. As all four doors burst open simultaneously, the music suddenly increased in volume. Four men jumped out of the car and headed toward me. In my surprised state, I did not have time to run, and they quickly surrounded me, pushing me toward their car.

Another car pulled up and a young Cambodian man threw open his car door, jumped out and shouted, "Let her go, she's my sister!" All four men hesitated for only a fraction of a second, just long enough for me to escape their grasp. I didn't know who he was or if he was any safer than the four men, but on impulse I jumped into his car and he followed. We sped off as I watched the other car drive in the opposite direction.

"You're safe now," he said, looking at me. "Sorry about the sister,thing. It was the only thing I could think of."

His quick thinking may well have saved my life, or at least my honor. If those men had managed to get me in their car, I am sure they would have raped and assaulted me, maybe even killed me. Sitting in this stranger's car, I realized that I was no safer in America than I had been in Cambodia.

As we drove away down PCH and my heart rate slowed, my savior, whose name was Paul, asked, "Where are you headed?" He must have assumed I was a runaway, because he did not ask me many questions.

Without thinking I said, "The Buddhist temple in Lakewood." *At least I will be safe there,* I thought.

I had never been to the temple, but had heard about it from Dr. Kong Chheng, a doctor at Chestnut. Lakewood was a neighboring city and only a few miles down the road, but at the time it seemed worlds away.

I lived in the temple for six months, sleeping in a tiny closet off one of the entrance doors, curled up in the corner like a frog. I rose at 4:00 every morning and made breakfast for the monks before getting a ride from one of the temple residents to school. I was happy to be able to continue attending classes at Hill Jr. High, despite its distance from my new home. The temple was actually a converted commercial building with many office-type rooms and a large assembly hall in the middle, a temporary location while a new temple in Long Beach was under construction. There were several saffron-robed monks living there and a committee of about twenty ladies who helped to manage temple affairs. One of them, a lady named Ma Keat, looked after me. She saw to it that my clothes were laundered, my sleeping space kept clean, and that there was always food saved for me to eat after riding the bus back from school. My days at the temple gave me a sense of security, which temporarily lifted me from my ongoing state of depression. I even considered becoming a nun so that I could stay there for the rest of my life.

During this time, one of my teachers at school read an article in the *L.A. Times* by a man named David Haldane and passed it on to me. Mr. Haldane had interviewed many Cambodians who escaped the killing fields of the Khmer Rouge genocide and were now living in Long Beach. The article focused on Asian-Americans living with the stress of cultural differences, and it was the first time I had seen something written about our plight. I was every person spoken of in that article; their hardships were my hardships. I was intrigued by the article and by the sense of purpose with which the author wrote.

At my teacher's request, I contacted Haldane, and we arranged to meet in front of a high school that wasn't too far away. He drove me to a restaurant where he interviewed me over a meal. It was the first time in my life I had ever shared my past with someone who had not experienced it for themselves, and I found it a great release. I did not mind answering his questions, but felt that my name should not be printed along with my story. He was very understanding and I trusted him fully.

My story ended up on the front page of the *Times.* The article has since been used in various Universities around the U.S. and has been published in a textbook called Cultural Tapestry: Readings for a Pluralistic Society (Harper Collins, 1992). Two other books have been published that contain the same article. Mr. Haldane was the first person in America to give me the chance to tell my story.

The Cambodian New Year was celebrated in the pagoda at the Lakewood temple. Cambodian people came from all over the city to celebrate the most important holiday of our times and to remember the day of the Khmer Rouge Invasion ten years earlier. Despite the horrible memories of the last New Year's celebration I had experienced, it was very encouraging to see the many Cambodian women dressed in traditional outfits. It was a moment of bittersweet joy among families, friends, and neighbors. There were toys for children and food for all. Everyone had fun playing traditional Cambodian games. I helped with one of the booths, collecting tickets and exchanging them for prizes. With the Cambodian New Year we celebrated the promise of generations to come and remembered that it takes strength, hope, and courage to cope with the many challenges we face, just as we do now.

A couple of months after I arrived at the temple, the new site was completed and the monks began to prepare for the move. By now, my presence had begun to cause problems among some of the older women on the temple committee. They were jealous of the attention I received from the monks and accused me of being a distraction. Ma Keat was not around at the time to defend me, and so the ladies of the committee took advantage of the move to throw me out. When I came home from school one day, I found my few possessions scattered on the sidewalk.

I was back on the streets again with nowhere to go. It was a wet, miserable evening, and I sat under a tree and watched the rain pour down just as I had done many times in the jungles of Cambodia. Other than my schoolbooks, the extent of my possessions were two spare sets of clothing, a backpack, one pair of underwear, and a pair of small, blue earrings.

I could not think of anywhere else to go, so I walked to the nearest phone booth and called information. I was given the address of a homeless shelter in Huntington Beach. After waiting in the rain at a bus stop, I paid my fare and rode the fifteen miles to my new home.

Upon arriving at the shelter, I was helped to dry off and given a secure place to sleep. I was also enrolled in a program for other teenagers like me—runaways and those who had never even had a place to runaway from. The program provided counseling to help me deal with the effects of both my past and recent experiences. I stayed for a few weeks in dorms with the others teens who were also experiencing difficult times. We were all of different cultural backgrounds, yet at the same time, we were very much alike. None of us had a home, and all of us were alone.

At the shelter, we sat in a circle for group therapy and talked about the good qualities we saw in one another. Here in this group, I learned the truth about myself and about who I was. I was complimented on my eyes and my lips, and told that I had a beautiful smile and lovely skin. I took a deep breath and thanked them. Though my guardians had cared for me greatly, I had never received this kind of affection or love before. I began to fully believe in my heart that I had a beautiful spirit and my inner self rejoiced.

Because of its distance from the shelter, I was unable to continue attending Hill Jr. High. My counselor at the shelter encouraged me to follow my heart and pursue my education, so I utilized all the resources in my power in order to do this. Yet according to Social Services, finding a home took priority over attending school, and I was not allowed to enroll in a school until my living situation was taken care of. Since I adamantly refused to return to Mrs. Touch, the social workers at the shelter were determined to find me a new home. I was placed in a series of unremarkable foster homes, none of which seemed particularly happy to see me. I had trouble accepting the different cultures, languages, foods, and attitudes of theses families and was labeled "uncooperative." I was ultimately placed in a group home in the city of La Verne, about sixty miles east of Long Beach, where I spent the next six months of my life.

A woman named Margaret ran this home for problem kids, gang members, and drug addicts. I had become somewhat bitter during my time in America and had become very street smart, sassy, and cynical. Needless to say, I fit in perfectly with the other kids at the home. Just as I learned how to stay alive in the jungles of Cambodia, I had learned how to survive the streets of urban America. It was about meeting pain and suffering head on and facing it with courage and a strong spirit. You had to be true to yourself, your roots, and your values. You could never show any weakness; it was important to act tough, no matter how scared you were. I pretended to know karate to keep the gang kids at bay. Figuring out ways to watch your own back was essential, and it was important to look out for others like yourself. Having a bad mouth and not being afraid to use it was another part of the act. If I backed down, even once, it would have been trouble. I gained respect as a crazy kid that no one messed with. Some of the white boys asked me how to say "I love you" in Khmer so they could pick up on Cambodian girls. Instead of telling them the right words, I told them to say A-krohk doech svaa. Some sra-laanh kha-nhom pong, which in Khmer means, "I am an ugly monkey. Please love me." It was to my great amusement that they were laughed at by the girls who they had tried to impress with their newly learned Khmer.

My rebelliousness was quickly broken, though, by Margaret's tough love. She strictly regulated the home, and our disciplined lifestyle helped shape my floating existence into a tangible thing. Everyone had duties to perform, and if you messed up, you lost movie privileges and had your weekly twenty dollar allowance docked. I found out that with good behavior, it was possible to transfer to Bonita High School, which offered a much better education than the one offered at the home. I set my mind on proving I should be transferred there and concentrated on following the rules and always kept my behavior in check. It took awhile, but my perseverance paid off, and I was able to convince Margaret that I was reformed enough to have a chance at a better education.

When I transferred to Bonita High School, I realized that it was sub-stantially different from Hill Jr. High. Bonita's academic standards were higher, and the teachers were more encouraging and supportive. One of the school's substitute teachers, a woman named Tracy, took a particular interest in me and spent time with me on the weekends, occasionally joining us for dinner at the home. With her support and mentoring, I began to do better in school. Tracy also helped me to petition the courts for my emancipation from Mrs. Touch, who was still legally my guard-ian even though I had an assigned social worker and did not receive any support from her.

I had lived in the group home for about four months when the court finally heard my case. Since I was only fifteen years old, I needed to find someone to live with until I could be fully emancipated at age sixteen. The only person that came to mind was Bang Soka. She and her husband had recently followed her mother and siblings to Long Beach and had moved into an apartment next door to theirs on Pacific Avenue. She agreed to let me stay with her and the court granted me permission to do so. Despite her mother's protests, she and her husband welcomed me into their home. She and her husband were very generous, but my staying there caused a rift to form between Soka, her mother, and her siblings. They hated her for letting me in and constantly bickered over my presence. But in the face of these arguments, she was kind enough to let me stay.

In 1988, on my sixteenth birthday, I was fully emancipated. It felt incredible to know that I was truly free from Mrs. Touch, but it was a hollow victory. I still felt empty inside and alone, and I always felt as if I was struggling just to survive.

I wanted to finish high school and had enrolled at Long Beach Polytechnic High. I chose Long Beach Poly because of its proximity to Bang Soka's apartment; I could walk to school rather than take the bus. This also made it easier for me to take an after school job bagging groceries and pushing carts at the Lucky's Supermarket that was within walking distance from the school. It was not a bad job, though on rainy days it was uncomfortable working outside in the cold, soaked through and pushing carts. But it wasn't nearly difficult as some of the other things I had been through, so I was grateful for the time it gave me to think and pray. I came to the conclusion that there was only one path for me—education would give me the tools to survive and the opportunities to lift myself up in the world. With education, I could do anything. I promised myself that I would not give up. I would pursue my education as far as I could.

One day, while waiting at a bus stop, I ran into a Cambodian friend who I had known in middle school. Her name was Ramsey, and I was very excited to see her.

"So, how are you?" I asked.

"Well, I'm okay, but my mother is sick, and we don't have the money to take her to the doctor. I've been out looking for a job all day, but haven't found one. I don't know what we're going to do," she said.

Ramsey's mother was widowed and taking care of her children in a crowded, two-bedroom apartment. She was frequently ill and made what money she could by telling fortunes and reading the palms of those who were desperate to know what the future held for them. I told her how my living with Bang Soka had divided the Touch family. Eventually, I grew bold enough to suggest that I move in with her and her family and help pay the rent. It would help her mother financially, Bang Soka would be able to make peace with her family, and I would be able to live with a friend I cared about. It seemed like it would be the best solution for us all. I moved in shortly thereafter, but not before having to break the news to Bang Soka.

CHAPTER THIRTEEN

Pomona

I woke up early the next morning before Soka or her husband and went to the kitchen to brew a pot of coffee. The sounds of percolation softly broke the stillness of the morning. I didn't know how to tell Soka that I was leaving. I did not want to appear ungrateful for all she had given me, but I knew I could no longer stay and be the cause of the fighting amongst her family. She was visibly upset by the constant bickering, and I knew it was hard for her to keep defending me. I wanted for her to have peace.

Just as the coffee pot machine clicked off, Soka entered the kitchen, fresh with the morning. "Good morning, Nga," she said. "Why are you up so early?"

"It's not early. It's seven. I was up at six. That's early." I poured the coffee into two cups. "I have to speak with you about something."

"What is it?" She took a seat at the kitchen table and sipped from her mug.

"I'm moving out." I looked down into the blackness of the coffee.

"Why?" she asked, stunned. "Are you not happy here?"

"I am very happy here, but I make things hard for you. I cause too many problems. Your mother hates me and so do your brothers and sisters," I said.

She set her mug down and reached across the table to grab my hand. "You are my sister, too. I don't care what they say. You can stay here as long as you want." She held my hand tightly.

"I must go, but you don't have to worry. I already have a place to stay. I hope you're not mad."

"No, I'm not," she said. "I know how stubborn you are, and I can tell that you have made up your mind about this. How can I stop you? If you ever need anything, please come back."

"Thank you for everything," I said.

We sat silently sipping our coffee, sad to see our time together come to an end.

Since Ramsey went to a different high school, I'd had to arrange for a ride to school and back everyday. One of my teachers, Megan, picked me up every morning for school and dropped me off at the apartment every afternoon. I needed to pay $250 to Ramsey's mother for rent every month, so I left Lucky's for a higher paying job at the T.G.&Y. clothing store. I worked hard for everything I had and saved as much as I could in my bank account. Things were going fine until one day, about a month after I had moved in. I came home after a long day at work to find Ramsey angry with me. She was upset because I had just taken on a second job at the Fabric Barn, while she had been unable to find a job for herself.

"I hate you!" she screamed. "You think you're so great with your two jobs, don't you?"

Many people had said many things to me in the past, but no one had ever said they hated me and the words cut deep.

"What are you talking about?" I asked. I hardly spoke of my jobs and certainly never bragged about money. I simply paid my rent on time every month, bought my groceries and clothing, and never asked for anything except a place to sleep.

"Shut up!" she screamed. She slung a slew of vulgarities at me, leaving me speechless. "You think you're a real hotshot. 'Look at me. I'm Nga and I've got tons of money!'" she said, mocking me. But I didn't feel any guilt or remorse—just sadness. I had no desire to wage a battle of words with her and so I kept silent.

"I never want to talk to you or see you again!" she screamed. "Get out of my house."

I didn't know what to say, but I didn't leave. I couldn't. I had nowhere else to go. My stomach twisted into knots. I just stood there, looking at her, waiting for her to stop screaming.

"You're impossible!" she said and stormed off to our room, slamming the door behind her.

As the apartment became quiet, I took a few deep breaths. Despite the fact that I was upset by Ramsey's attack, I was soon overwhelmed by stomach pains. I hadn't eaten since breakfast, had worked after school, and then gone to the bank to deposit a paycheck—all on an empty stomach. The pain in my gut was unbearable, and I had to settle my stomach before attempting to settle things with Ramsey. I went to the kitchen to look for something to eat. Ramsey's mother had made some chicken soup earlier that day and left it on the countertop. I ate directly from the container, not wanting to waste time scooping some into a bowl.

After swallowing a few mouthfuls, my stomach began to feel worse. I was overcome by a horrible headache and a fuzzy dizziness penetrated my vision. A wave of nausea forced me to run to the bathroom where I vomited repeatedly. The room spun around me, and I broke into a cold sweat. I was soaked in perspiration and began to shiver uncontrollably. The room kept spinning until my eyes rolled back in my head and I fainted.

I eventually came to and was able to crawl from the bathroom to our bedroom. Ramsey was no longer there, and as far as I could tell, the apartment was empty. Once in bed, I passed out a second time.

It must have been hours later when I woke up and a few more passed before I stopped shivering and shaking.

Ramsey's mother came into the room. "Nga," she said, "are you feeling better? We were so worried about you."

"I'm feeling a little better, but I feel very weak," I said, sitting up slowly. The fogginess in my head had not yet dissipated entirely.

"Well, when you can get up, come into the living room. I have something that will help you feel better." She smiled a queer smile, almost as if she were a little afraid of me, but didn't want to show it. Then she backed out of the room and shut the door.

A while later, I ventured into the living room where she began to chant over me. My initial impulse was to resist her chanting. I had never felt comfortable with her fortune telling and other strange religious practices and became especially uncomfortable when she began to direct her spells at me.

"I think I'll be okay now," I said and stood up to go back to my bedroom. Ramsey and her brother stepped into the room and blocked the doorway, preventing me from leaving.

"Stay right here. I'm not finished," her mother said.

She bit off a piece of chewing tobacco and spit the juice in my face. I was shocked and repulsed.

"What are you doing?" I asked, backing away and wiping the brown ooze from my cheek.

"You're sick. We need to get the evil out."

"I just have the flu or something. There's no evil in me."

"You were saying things in your delirium. Evil things. This is not the flu," she said.

She resumed her chanting as Ramsey's older brother took hold of me. I tried to free myself from his grasp, but he was too strong. I was still weak and confused from my illness, and I didn't have the strength to fight back. He dragged me downstairs as Ramsey and her mother followed. They forced me into the backseat of their car and the four of us started driving.

No one would say where we were going, and the only sound in the car came from Ramsey's mother who continued to chant. No one would look at me. Besides fortune telling and some strange prayers, I had never noticed them do anything that seemed out of the ordinary, but now I felt that I was in the midst of something very evil.

A large sign on the side of the road welcomed us to the city of Pomona, about 40 miles from Long Beach. I was chilled and sweating, shivering in my fever, and the rough driving only added to my nausea. The car finally stopped in front of a house with an overgrown lawn. There was a tall, chain link fence surrounding the house, and just inside the fence was a Cambodian man, dressed in black. The windows of the house were secured with iron bars and the door was secured by a heavy, wrought iron gate.

"What is this place?" I asked.

No one answered. Instead, her brother got out, opened the door and grabbed my arm. The man unlocked the fence and the front door for us, and we filed into the house. It was dark inside and smelled of mildew and incense.

When my eyes adjusted to the dim light of the room, I couldn't believe what I saw. The living room had been turned into some sort of shrine, unlike any other shrine I had ever seen. A large statue of Buddha sat in the center of the room and next to it was a high platform with a golden throne. Upon it sat a Vietnamese woman with gray hair, wrapped in silk robes. Her position upon the throne implied that she believed herself to be Buddha's queen, an angel-god of sorts, and the other people in the house who were kneeling and sitting before her obviously agreed.

My heart raced in panic. This was not the Buddhism I knew. This had been tainted by the occult, and I was sickened by it. Ramey's brother pulled me toward the woman. She looked at me, touched my clammy forehead, chanted something in Vietnamese and then said to me, "You are a ghost in your own body. Your mind has been corrupted, but you are here now, and we can help you."

I wanted no part of her supposed cure. I said, "There's something wrong with all of you. You're crazy." I began to feel faint.

"We are instruments of our god. You must trust us."

"This is not the way of Buddha! You are not saints!" I screamed at them.

I felt a blow to the back of my knees. I fell to the ground and was attacked from all sides. I was held and beaten. Through the chaos around me, the woman in silk brought a white candle to my head and singed my hair at the roots. I had not acknowledged them as godly, and so they attempted to beat me into submission. I lost and regained consciousness repeatedly and only remember seeing Ramsey and her family dancing and chanting with the others. They were instruments of the devil, not God, and it was destroying them. I blacked out.

It must have been the next day when I finally woke up. I was lying on the dirty floor of a small, dark room. I felt around in the dark for a doorknob, and when I found it, it was locked. I continued searching with my hands until I found a light switch. I flipped it on to see that my makeshift prison cell was actually a large closet, empty except for some trash that had been swept into the corners. I examined myself, prepared to see great damage as a result of the beatings. I was weak and my body ached, but nowhere on my body did any marks appear. *Did I imagine it all?* I thought.

I looked myself over, and despite the beating I remembered, I had no bruises or cuts. I reached to my forehead where the flame had singed my hair and felt nothing. Nothing, because my hair was gone. They had shaved my head and locked me in a closet. Although I could not explain the lack of bruising, I knew it had all happened just as I remembered it. I still felt feverish and the heat of it seemed to burn through my skull. My flushed body was drenched in sweat. I was completely isolated.

I was kept in the closet for what must have been a week. I did not see Ramsey or her mother again, and I was given little food to eat. I just sat, cried, and prayed that God would save me.

The ones who gave me my meals were Cambodian or Vietnamese. I could hear their chanting through the locked door, but could only understand parts of what they said. It was if they had made up a language all their own. From what I could tell, they were thanking their god for the virgin he had brought them and prayed for her recovery and purification. The idea that virginal young women are pure and share a special spiritual connection with the gods is a common belief in eastern religions. I knew I was their virgin. I did not fear that they would kill me, as they believed it more to their benefit to use me. They hoped I would become one of them and channel their spirits and gods. I prayed to God that he would save me from these people who were so misguided in their religion.

I thought back over all the events I had survived up to that point. *They may have locked me inside this house,* I thought, *but my fate is still my own.* I continued to pray, asking God to provide a means of escape. I felt compelled to try the knob on the door to the closet, and it turned in my hand. I opened the door.

I let the bright light from the room bathe my wounded spirit and guide me to where I belonged. I did not know how I would escape, but believed I was being led to my freedom. I had been blessed with many miracles before this, and I knew that if I had faith, I would escape yet again. I walked cautiously through the house, but it appeared to be empty. I headed for the door and tried the knob. Like the closet door, it, too, was unlocked. As I crossed the threshold, a strong, intangible force pulled me back. I struggled against it, walking away from the house as fast as I could.

I walked until I came to a bus stop. I was surprised to find that I still had some money in my pocket as well as my ID and bank book, but there wasn't enough to take a bus anywhere. Not knowing what else to do, I called my teacher, Megan.

"Where have you been?" she asked. "I came to get you for school every day this week and no one answered the door."

I looked at my faint reflection in the glass of the phone booth and saw my shaved head. "I'm in trouble," I said. "I need you to come get me."

When she arrived at the bus station, she was shocked by my appearance. "Who did this to you?" she asked.

"Ramsey and her family. They beat me and locked me in a room." I was embarrassed and certain that she would not believe such a wild story.

"Then we should go to the police," she said. She looked at me, but not with compassion or caring. She looked at me with fear. She was afraid of me.

"No. I don't want to do that." I did not look like I had been beaten, burned, and practically starved. I had no bruises or scars. I looked like a runaway kid who had shaved her head in a fit of rebellion and then made up a wild story of kidnap and torture for attention. At least that's what I thought they would see. It seemed that was what Megan saw.

We drove back to Long Beach in silence. I could feel her tension and her desire to be rid of me. It was evening when we arrived at the United Cambodian Center, a resource center for immigrants who had gotten mixed up in gangs. It was the only place I could think of for her to take me to. I didn't want to bother Bang Soka, as I had caused her enough trouble as it was. But the UCC was closed when we got there and so, albeit reluctantly, Megan took me home with her.

She gave me some sheets and a pillow and told me I could shower and then sleep on the couch. As I let the warm water wash the terror of the last week away, I knew in my heart that Megan did not trust me. I spent the night on her sofa, and in the morning she dropped me off at the UCC. They were mostly a gang outreach facility and could do nothing except to refer me back to social services. I called Megan, hoping she would let me stay another night at her house, but she would no longer accept my calls. She was afraid of me.

"Thank you for everything you have done for me. I appreciate it very much," I said into her answering machine, and then hung up the phone.

CHAPTER FOURTEEN

Graduation

I called up a girl I had met about three months earlier. I had been out for a walk one day when I passed by a Christian church where a young adult Bible study was taking place. I joined their discussion, eager to learn everything I could about the Christian faith as I was inspired by their values of compassion and unconditional love.

Her name was Yelna, and she came to my aid when I needed her. She was a college student I had met at the Bible study and I had kept up a friendly acquaintance with her. Upon learning that I was largely on my own, she had given me her number. I was very glad that I had memorized it.

"What happened to your hair?" she asked as I got into her car.

"These crazy religious fanatics tried to make me join their cult," I said, laughing a little in an attempt to brush it off as nothing too serious.

"And you let them shave your head?" She was incredulous.

"Not exactly . . ." I said, trailing off, hoping I would not have to explain in detail.

She must have sensed my apprehension of talking about it and instead of pushing me for details simply said, "Well, unless you like the bald look, we need to buy you a wig."

Using money I had withdrawn from the bank, I purchased a black wig that made me look somewhat normal again, although I knew the kids at school were bound to make fun of me. I didn't care, though. I just wanted to get on with my life.

"You can move in with my grandmother. She lives on Walnut Street. It's not the greatest area, but it's a place to stay," Bang Yelna said, and she was right. Gang members gathered in the street in front of her house—the looming threat of impending violence. Helicopters thundered frequently through the skies and sirens were heard so often that we often stopped hearing them. Yelna's grandmother was a devout Christian and took me to church with her every evening. I soon found myself helping with the services and going door-to-door with her as she spread the gospel.

I had been right in assuming that the kids at school would make fun of me. They spread rumors that I was crazy. Megan ignored me at school, and I kept to myself as much as I could.

These many years of suffering caused me to value life more than most and gave me the ability to offer unconditional love more readily than most. The difficult times I experienced during my childhood proved highly valuable to my future. I began to work as a volunteer at the UCC, helping ex-gang members, pregnant teenage girls, and other kids with their homework. It felt good to be helping people who had experienced many of the same things I had. I could relate to them on a very personal level. Yet despite this, these kinds of experiences, though similar, are at the same time very singular. During this time I gained valuable experience and knowledge, my capacity for compassion increased, and I worked hard to strengthen my economic independence. I also learned a lot about the importance of raising awareness among diverse communities. Many Cambodians struggled with a language barrier that made it difficult for them to get the help they needed. I longed so much for the return of our Khmer culture that seemed to have faded when we immigrated to the US. I began to believe that a revival of our history and culture would help to ease the fears and loneliness that we faced as new American immigrants. Through my volunteer work, I was able to earn the trust of many scared Cambodians, and in the process I found a place for myself where I was useful. It was my first experience giving something back to the Cambodian community, and I found it highly rewarding.

One day, my school guidance counselor called me into her office. I walked in, nervous and under the impression that I was in some kind of trouble.

"Please sit down," she said.

"Thank you," I said as I sat in a hard, wooden chair in front of her desk.

She looked at me with compassion and smiled. "You know, you are a lucky student." She smiled and handed me a few pieces of notebook paper that had been stapled together. It was an essay I had written about my life and academic goals for one of my ESL classes.

"This essay won you a scholarship."

"A scholarship?" I asked, unsure of what she meant.

"Money for college. Like I said, you're very lucky. It's enough for at least two years at the community college."

My heart leapt in my chest. College! I hadn't even begun to think about what I would do after graduation. I spent most of my time just trying to forget what had happened with Ramsey and trying to remember my homework assignments. But now, I didn't have to worry—high school would end, but my education would continue. I felt very blessed.

Knowing I had a scholarship waiting for me didn't make getting through those final weeks of high school any easier. At times, it seemed as though I would never make it. Speaking and reading English continued to be a difficulty, and it took a lot of hard work to get through my final exams at Long Beach Poly. Many nights I cried myself to sleep, overloaded and exhausted from the constant struggle to support myself. But that year, in 1991, I graduated from high school. Over five hundred families attended the graduation ceremony to celebrate the success of their children. The fact that I had no family to share my success with only served to emphasize my loneliness. The graduating seniors were all invited to attend a grad night party in the gym after the ceremony, but I didn't feel as if I belonged there. After receiving my diploma, I went home and cried myself to sleep, yet again. I had not felt the sense of accomplishment that I had expected would accompany graduation. Had I been able to share this with Mother and Father Voung, Chandra Sam or the Sarims, perhaps I would have felt differently. I know they would have looked on at the graduation ceremony with great pride.

Chapter Fifteen

College

In August of 1991, I moved out of the apartment of Bang Yelna's grandmother and was able to rent an apartment of my own on Atlantic Avenue. I began classes at Long Beach City College, but I was somewhat unprepared for the demanding standards of higher education. I still struggled with my English skills; I had trouble pronouncing words clearly and missed the meaning of many of the things I read in my textbooks. I dedicated myself to mastering the basics of communication, so I challenged myself by taking drama and speech classes. Drama classes helped me improve my ability to express myself nonverbally, through body language and facial expressions, while speech classes gave me confidence to speak in front of my peers. My professors praised my natural abilities in these areas, but encouraged me to push myself beyond my comfort zone. I was still somewhat shy and had developed the bad habits of stuffing my hands in my pockets and keeping my head down while I spoke.

"No one will listen to what you have to say unless you say it with conviction. So get your hands out of your pockets, stand up straight, and say what you want to say," a professor once told me.

I took his advice and my classmates began to show great interest in what I had to say. Though I gave many speeches and performed many roles, what I never told anyone was that I drew my inspiration from my personal experiences. When I spoke about homelessness, no one knew that I had been homeless myself. When I spoke about war, no one would have ever guessed that just a few years earlier I had been in the middle of one. When a role in drama class required me to cry, I never told anyone that the tears came from the memories of those I had lost. These things were very much a part of me, and I was still extremely protective of my identity. Nonetheless, coming from a culture that values oral history as a means to pass on traditions, I appreciated the value of enlightening others through oral communication and did the best I could to share my experiences with them.

My dream was to transfer to a four-year university where I would be able to study international relations. I hoped to get a master's degree and then pursue a law degree. Growing up in a society that had been unable to rule itself without the interference of foreign governments gave me the desire to be politically active. I hoped that one day I would be in a position to change the direction of Cambodia's future by helping to write the first Khmer Constitution. Or perhaps I would pursue a journalistic career, writing articles about the real stories of life—the ones that heighten public awareness and change the world, not celebrity gossip or fluff. They were ambitious goals and still a long way off, but I tried not to give up hope. I had made it this far. What could stop me now?

I had left my jobs at T.G.&Y. and The Fabric Barn in order to work closer to the college campus. During the week, I tutored students from the local elementary schools in math (at which I excelled) and worked as a housekeeper. On the weekends, I worked from five in the morning until midnight at the Long Beach Boulevard Donut Shop. The days were long and sometimes boring, and I had plenty of time to fantasize about what I would do if I hadn't had to work constantly. Free time was a rarity, but should it ever materialize, I wanted to be ready for it with a great plan. While daydreaming at the donut shop one day, I was fantasizing about leaving the store and searching for a better job. I longed to work in a place that did not require me to be on my feet all day long. On this particular day, the store was quiet and hardly anyone had been in all day. The air was thick and stifling, and I longed for something to happen that would break the stillness. A distinguished-looking man who slightly resembled Ronald Reagan walked into the shop. He had the same slicked-back hair, angular shoulders, and broad, friendly smile as the former President. He wore a smart business suit and looked far too wealthy to be in a donut shop. He should have been eating French pastries in a penthouse office with a Pacific Ocean view. Having been alone in the shop all day, I was excited to have someone to talk to, even if all we talked about was whether he wanted a jelly-filled or glazed.

"I'd like an old-fashioned, please. And a coffee," he said, reaching for his wallet.

"How are you today?" I asked as I directed a pair of tongs into the donut case toward the last buttermilk donut.

"Well, I'm definitely not having a good day." He gave a wry smile as he said this, but I could tell that he wasn't joking. He stood at the counter and began to talk about his family troubles and financial worries. I had only been looking for some idle conversation, not someone's sob story. After all, I had my own sob story and was still trying to deal with it. I tried to change the subject.

"Has anyone ever told you that you look like President Reagan?" I asked, knowing well how much flattery can achieve.

"No. No one ever has. But I am close friends with Ron, so maybe a little of his good looks have rubbed off on me."

I was impressed. "Wow! You know Ronald Reagan?" I handed him his donut.

"We go way back to when he was running for governor. In fact, I'm the reason he became a Republican," he said with another grin.

I didn't understand his joke, and I didn't want to ask him to explain it. What I did want was for him to leave and not bother me anymore. I began to wish I was alone with my own miseries again. He eventually left, but he continued to come in every Saturday and Sunday to see me and to eat his old-fashioned and drink his coffee. He was always trying to give me advice, and I thought that he just talked too much in general, but I did my best to put up with him.

His name was Robert Lewis Simpson, but he said that most people called him Bob. He had a certain air of greatness about him, and I thought he was too distinguished to be simply called Bob. As time passed, we became firm breakfast buddies, chatting as he enjoyed his coffee and donut.

Refugees from war-torn areas such as Cambodia arrive in America trying to forget, hoping above all for the simple pleasure of living in peace and freeing themselves from fear. Unfortunately for some, the

torture never ends. I have heard that An Chan, a survivor of the Cambodian genocide once said, "I was free in America but my mind was still a
slave." I felt the same. No matter how hard I tried to forget, I was a slave
to my memories. However, Mr. Simpson helped me out of that terrible
place. Through his friendship and his firm guidance, he provided me
with an opportunity to redirect my life in a new and positive direction.
He showed me how to turn the nightmares from the past into dreams
for the future by training me in the skills of social and political activism. This great man showed me how even one person with inspiration,
patience, and firm determination can make a difference to the world
they live in.

He was kind and spoke to me as if I were his equal. Once, he
asked me what I planned to do in the future.

"All I want is to be an ordinary girl and to lead a simple life," I
said.

He looked at me seriously. "That's a shame, because you are not
a normal girl, and you will never be able to lead a simple life. You are
beautiful, inside and out, and have so much potential. To strive for the
ordinary would be to waste it all."

I grew uncomfortable with his compliments and quickly changed
the subject, but his words struck deep. I decided that if I wanted things
to change, I could not keep waiting for them to change on their own. I
needed to take action. Someone needed to uncover the truth about the
plight of Cambodian immigrants, and I was going to be that person.

As our friendship grew, I discovered that he was a lawyer, but that he
also worked in real estate and investments. He had recently purchased
the grocery store next door to the donut shop, and since I was always
looking for an opportunity to earn additional income, I asked him if he
would be interested in hiring me as a clerk.

"Of course. It's time you get out of this donut shop. But I'd rather
you help me out with my law practice. I think you're more suited for
working with the law than bagging groceries," he said.

He graciously offered to take me on as his legal assistant, and he taught me how to perform Internet research and paralegal work; skills that would later prove useful in my work for the Long Beach Cambodian community. We made a good team, and Mr. Simpson won a number of cases while we worked together. He was keen for me to develop what he saw as potential leadership skills. "You are young and capable and can do valuable work for the Cambodian community," he once said.

But no matter how bad I wanted to become involved, it was hard to believe that I could make any sort of difference. "No matter how civilized and honest politics appear," I argued, "deep down it seems it's always laced with deceit and betrayal."

He looked at me intently. "If you want to change the system, you must first know the system. You will do well to learn everything you can about politics so as to use it to your advantage."

Mr. Simpson had a theory that there was a recurring model in history that could bring about political and social change in any country, when properly used. It began with a few highly principled, very committed people who were prepared to risk everything for the sake of their common beliefs. They were very educated, dedicated, courageous, and fiercely loyal to each other and their cause. This small circle of people eventually grew, gradually building up a momentum sufficiently powerful enough to effect change. Using the founding of America by a small group of Europeans dedicated to independence as an example, he encouraged me to pursue this model in my activism for Cambodia. For the first time, I began to see the possibility of changing things in my country. Until then, it had all seemed hopeless—an impossible task. But Mr. Simpson succeeded in opening a door to new possibilities for me. As we spent more time together, my intellectual horizons started to widen, and my mind, dull for so long, began to awaken.

During this period, I filed my application for U.S. citizenship, and in 1992, I was sworn in as a U.S. citizen. I was ready to trade the stigma of being a refugee for the honor of being an American. I was now dedicated to looking forward, and so to put the past behind me, I chose a new name for myself. I had gone by many names in my life, all of which had suited me at the time I used them. Although the name I had been using, Sophorn, was precious and the only thing I had left from the Sarim family, I needed to start fresh. I used syllables from the names of all the people who had helped me survive and combined them to form a new name—Oni Vitandham. It was a sign of a new beginning, and the depression that had been hanging over me for the past few years began to lift. I began to look at life in a more positive and optimistic light, but there were still many difficult challenges to face.

Robert Lewis Simpson was born in Oklahoma in 1921. He had served in the Air Force during World War II with former President George Bush. He had piloted a B-17 bomber and had flown over Germany dropping American bombs. The blood of innocent civilians stained his hands, but he was proud that he had served his country. Beyond this, he also had his own reasons for participating in the war. He felt a personal obligation to do what he could to free the world from poverty, so he attempted to do this the only way that he knew how—by joining the military.

"Sometimes, war is the only way to fix certain problems," he once told me. "Joining the Air Force was one of the most difficult decisions I ever had to make, but without war, there could be no liberty, no justice, and no real social change would ever take place."

When he returned home from the war, he began to think about his future and his family. He wanted to raise his children in a country they could be proud of. He saw a great future for the United States of America, and he wanted to be a part of it. He was a good friend of Richard Nixon when he was preparing to run for the United States Senate in 1968. Mr. Simpson told me how he encouraged Nixon to seek a larger public role and urged him to run for President. Mr. Simpson played a vital role in the organization of a fundraising campaign for Nixon's White House bid.

"We even sold hot dogs in the park to raise extra money," he said. "We wanted to show America that an ordinary man could become the President."

I admired his unwavering belief in the power of a single person—

a seemingly ordinary person—to make significant social changes. He believed Nixon could change America and did everything he could to get him into office. When Nixon won the 1968 Presidential election, he appointed Mr. Simpson to join his administration in Washington. Mr. Simpson declined, choosing to stay in California with his family instead.

He remained in close contact with President Nixon and was one of the few people to offer counsel on difficult policy decisions made by Nixon during his Presidency, including the controversial decision to bomb Cambodia in 1970. When he told me about his involvement with this event, I was completely shocked. I did not understand how Mr. Simpson, a man I had come to admire and respect, could have helped to order the killing of all my innocent countrymen.

It upset me so much that I was unable to sleep for weeks. I started having nightmares about everything that I witnessed while living in Cambodia. I blamed Mr. Simpson for my sorrow and depression. I felt anger in my heart as I realized how many Khmer citizens died in the bombing that had opened the doors for the Khmer Rouge takeover. It was an odd coincidence for people from opposite sides of the conflict to meet as Mr. Simpson and I did, and it seemed nearly impossible to me that we could remain friends now that we knew of the roles we had unknowingly played in each other's lives.

CHAPTER SIXTEEN

Motherhood

On a Saturday in April of 1993, I paid my weekly visit to a Thai Buddhist temple near my apartment. There was a Cambodian monk there who had been raised in Thailand and whom I enjoyed spending time with. He introduced me to a young Cambodian man named Phal Kam who was from a wealthy and well-known family in Cambodia and who had recently come to America to study. He asked me to assist him in finding a place to live. By now, I was used to doing such work in the community and was happy to help. Right from the beginning, however, I was unsure of Phal Kam. He was short and unattractive, but there was something else about him, something that made me unsure of his intentions. It didn't take long for Phal Kam to prove that my suspicions were correct. He began to follow me and was always around every corner I approached, whether at school or work. I tried to explain to him that I was not interested in being anything more than friends, but he did not desist.

One evening Phal Kam came to my apartment, bringing with him a takeout dinner for both of us. I was wary of spending time together, but when he showed up with food in hand, I felt that I could not turn him away. He left after we finished the meal, but he returned shortly thereafter claiming to have forgotten his keys. After a few moments, it was clear he had not returned for his keys—he had returned for me. He grabbed my arm, caressed my face, and tried to kiss me. I attempted to push him away, but he was strong and determined. I was forcefully raped and left lying on the floor of my own apartment. My clothes were torn, and I could feel the hot sting of tears on my face. The shame I felt was unbearable. Weeks passed before I could leave my apartment; I could not face my friends at school nor my coworkers, and I was simply too afraid to tell anyone about Phal Kam.

Shortly thereafter, I began to feel tired and ill. My head ached constantly, and I spent most mornings vomiting in the bathroom. I was so innocent about these matters that I did not recognize the signs of pregnancy. After three months of constant nausea, I walked into Long Beach Memorial Hospital and waited to see a doctor. The diagnosis of pregnancy was heartbreaking, and I panicked at the prospect of being an unwed mother. Being a poor college student, working full-time and being utterly alone, there was no way I could properly raise a baby, and the scorn I would face in the Cambodian community was too much to imagine. I felt that I had no other choice than to abort the child. I had not been a willing partner to Phal Kam. In my panicked state of mind, abortion seemed the only way out.

I remembered hearing an old wives' tale that said that you could abort a baby by consuming a large quantity of alcohol, so I began drinking as much wine as I could, hoping it would precipitate a miscarriage. After four weeks, I was still pregnant, and my panic only increased with the passage of time. I bought five bottles of wine at the supermarket, took them home, and started drinking. I had swallowed the contents of one bottle and was feeling terrible when something miraculous happened. A voice in my head spoke to me very clearly.

Do not do this, it told me. *This is a human life. This baby is meant to come and live with you.* I recognized it as being the same voice I had heard many years before, in Phnom Penh, the one that had urged me to go to Angkor Wat. However, this time I was too afraid to listen. I grabbed the second bottle and started drinking, trying to drown out the voice. Suddenly, the bottle was knocked out of my hand by an unseen force. It fell to the floor and smashed apart, its dark red contents staining the carpet. Again, the voice inside me spoke. *Do not harm this child.* Still, I ignored the voice and grabbed for another bottle. But before I could reach them, all three remaining bottles spontaneously cracked apart and the wine spilled out onto the floor. I collapsed on the floor and slipped into unconsciousness.

I eventually regained consciousness with my heart pounding and my entire body shaking. After the mysterious events of the previous night, I gave up all attempts to abort the child growing inside me. The next day I returned to Long Beach Memorial. To my astonishment, the ultrasound showed that I was carrying twins. My heart dropped when I learned this. I now had every intention of keeping the babies, but I felt completely at a loss. How could I provide for two babies and Phal Kam when I could barely provide for myself? I prayed to God that he would give me the ability to be a strong mother. I survived only on the faith that these children were coming to me for a reason.

Phal Kam moved in with me as soon as I told him that I was pregnant with twins. He was not eager to become a father, but took advantage of the situation in order to live with me. In our tradition, the father of your child is family whether you are married or not, and I felt that it was my duty to do everything in my power to make our family work. We lived together as man and wife, although we never made our marriage legal by American law.

Phal Kam expected me to work hard through my pregnancy, but I had fallen out of contact with Mr. Simpson and no longer worked with him. It was difficult for me to face him knowing that he had played such an active part in the fate of my country, and so I resumed working at the donut shop.

Phal Kam had no job and no apparent intention of getting one. Living with him was like losing everything that I worked so hard to achieve, and I lost all confidence in myself. We soon found ourselves unable to pay rent and the landlord of our building evicted us, leaving us homeless for a short while. Phal Kam's behavior toward me became increasingly violent. He beat me even though I was pregnant. I fell into a severe depression as once again, everything in my life began to seem hopeless.

"If you tell anyone," he said, "your life will pay the forfeit." I was terrified of the harm he was capable of inflicting upon me and my unborn children, so I kept his secrets.

In the fourth month of my pregnancy, I experienced the consequences of the combination of my early attempts at abortion and Phal Kam's beatings. Early one morning, intense pain ripped through my abdomen, and I became feverish and faint. Somehow I made it to the bathroom, where I passed a significant amount of blood. The possibility of a miscarriage, a possibility that I had once hoped for, now filled me terror. Both babies were apparently lost, having succumbed to the alcohol and violence I had subjected them to. Sitting on the bathroom floor, covered in blood, I was overcome with guilt and fear. *God, I know I made the wrong choice, but it was before I knew your plan. Please forgive me!* I thought. I knew I would have to tell Phal Kam, so I cleaned myself up and went to him. When I told him, he simply looked at me and said nothing.

Slowly, the abdominal cramps subsided and I was able to return to work. I had expected to feel different—I had expected to feel a hole in my womb where the babies had slept. But my first day back at the donut shop, I still felt very much pregnant. It was as if one of the babies was still inside me, struggling to survive. I prayed that this would be true, and over the next few months, my belly continued to grow. I was incredibly thankful for the miracle God had given me.

During one of my later appointments at Long Beach Memorial, it was confirmed that I had lost one of the babies, but tests showed that the surviving child was still growing. The miscarriage was quietly noted in my medical record, and never mentioned again.

I was scrubbing the floors at the donut shop when I went into labor two months premature. The labor was extremely painful, and my daughter was underweight and sickly. We were both kept at the hospital for four days, until we were strong enough to return home. Phal Kam came to visit us in the hospital, but it was difficult for me to recognize him as the father of my beautiful gift from God.

Although I felt extremely apprehensive about having a child, I am so thankful that God intervened and stopped me from aborting my daughter. I named her Reachiny, which means "queen" in Khmer. She brought a kind of love into my life I had never before experienced. She became my best friend, as well as my daughter. We looked after and protected each other. She was bright, intelligent, beautiful, and truly a gift from God.

CHAPTER SEVENTEEN

Progressive United Action Association
The Foundation For Cambodia

Never doubt that a small group of thoughtful,
committed citizens can change the world: indeed it's
the only thing that ever has.—Margaret Mead

I had taken a job working at a jewelry store in the Long Beach Mall, and was living in an apartment on Sherman Place with Phal Kam and Reachiny, when I had a chance reunion with Mr. Simpson while waiting in line at a local Bank of America branch. We were both surprised and delighted to see each other again, and we resolved to remain in touch. We began to meet regularly for lunch, and Mr. Simpson said he was looking forward to revisiting our dialogue on how to help the situation in Cambodia.

Over lunch one day he said, "You should try to create a core group of like-minded people who will work together to plan a new future for Cambodia."

"But how do I do that?" I was very interested in doing something of that nature, but it seemed like a huge task, and I had no idea where to begin.

"You can start by going door-to-door. Talk to people. Get to understand their needs. Let them know that it's time for them to be heard." He told me that once I understood their needs, I could then bring those needs to the attention of policy makers and government leaders through a letter writing campaign. "No policy has ever been changed," he said, "without some history of lobbying for or against it."

"It still seems overwhelming," I said.

"Don't worry. Start small. Just get to know one person at a time. But most importantly, follow your heart."

I was in the habit of going down to the ocean after work each day. It gave me a chance to get my thoughts in order and to escape the domestic turmoil I was constantly faced with at home. The rock walls lining the harbor reminded me of the place in Kompong Som where Chandra Sam had died. One such day, as I stared out over the Pacific Ocean, I was inspired to compose a letter to President Clinton regarding human rights abuses in Cambodia. I went home and drafted a letter to show to Mr. Simpson. It was a pretty basic letter, but he was delighted with it, so I sent copies to the President, the United Nations, and Senator Jesse Helms, who was then the head of the U.S. Foreign Relations Committee.

Soon I was sending out hundreds of letters a month and collecting replies, most of which were form letters. But the lack of personal replies did not leave me discouraged. Mr. Simpson had told me that the process would be slow and that the chance of gaining immediate results was unlikely, but I knew it was a start. Gradually, one letter at a time, progress was made.

There is a story in the East about a seagull whose eggs wash out of her nest on the beach and into the ocean. She demands that the ocean return her eggs, but the mighty ocean just laughs back at her. She threatens to drain the ocean dry unless it responds to her demands. Again, the sea laughs at her. So she starts to empty the ocean one sip at a time, picking up the water in her beak and dumping it on the beach. It seemed an impossible task, but she would not give up. Gradually, all the other creatures, impressed by her courage and determination, came to her aid. Soon there was such an army of animals and birds helping in her task that the ocean, fearful of the combined effort against it, relented and returned the eggs with the next tide. I became that seagull; I wrote to Presidents, foreign ministers, senators, heads of relief organizations, U.N. officials, anyone I could think of who could possibly help me change the mind of the mighty political ocean. I was just one lonely voice, but I knew if I persisted, I would find others who would join me.

Meanwhile, I began networking in the local Cambodian community. Working in the jewelry store allowed me to save enough money to purchase two donut stores, which I ran without much help from Phal Kam. One, called Amy's Donuts, was on Knott Avenue in the city of Cypress, about eleven miles away from Long Beach. The other one was Dolly's Donuts, located on Woodruff Street in Bellflower, another neighboring city. Soon an awareness of my efforts spread among the local Cambodians, and people began calling the store to ask for advice on all kinds of matters, including legal, family, and immigration problems. I wrote letters to the mayor of Long Beach to obtain help for victims of gang violence and drive-by shootings. I petitioned the State Department about social security and welfare reform. I worked on divorces, child custody cases, and domestic violence cases—I did anything and everything I could to help the people who had come to depend on me.

Mr. Simpson, meanwhile, was spending a lot of time his own time working on behalf of the local Cambodians. He loved our food, especially the spicy rice and fish soup that we traditionally eat for breakfast. "It keeps me healthy," he would say. He would spend countless hours in Cambodian restaurants, sitting around and talking with the workers and patrons whenever he could, continually urging them to be strong and to fight for their country with their voices.

One of the main obstacles that we were constantly up against was the lack of unity among the Cambodians themselves, and this remains one of the biggest problems still facing the community today. A community divided is always weak, but distrust and fear, bred in the minds of Cambodians by the Khmer Rouge, had traveled to America with us. Until we mended those divisions, it would be impossible to attract the kind of support we needed. With Mr. Simpson's encouragement, I decided to start an organization that would represent my desire to bring all Cambodians together. I called it Progressive United Action Association (PUAA): Progressive because I wanted us, as a culture, to move forward; United, because I wanted us to work together; and Action, because we needed to do something in order to create progress and unity.

I had a clear vision of the purpose of PUAA: to improve the condition of life for all Cambodians; to fight the problems of human rights violations, injustice, child abuse and land mines; to create a democratic government and a just legal system in Cambodia; to provide education about HIV/AIDS; and to provide a proper system of public education. Furthermore, I wanted the association to act as a bridge between the diverse cultures of Cambodia, between the new generation and the old generation, and even more importantly, between the Cambodians who came to America and those who stayed behind. I wanted to solve the problem of illiteracy in Cambodia and encourage the growth of science and technology in order to bring about a better quality of life. I wanted to firmly establish the principles of liberty, peace, justice, and decency in the hearts of all Cambodians, whether they lived in Cambodia or America.

I threw myself into my work; all my energies were focused on this new endeavor. It felt as if I had been reborn, and I was filled with anticipation for the success that I believed was inevitable.

I will never forget my first public presentation. I received an invitation to speak in Fresno, California, the home of another sizeable Cambodian community. I was nervous and highly intimidated, but I had not lost my determination, and I intended to see it through no matter what it took. I boarded a Greyhound bus to Fresno on April 12, 1997. It rained heavily that day, unusual weather for California, and it reminded me of the tropical monsoon storms common in Cambodia. I remembered that I often had to trudge through those storms while fleeing the Khmer Rouge patrols and the memory somehow strengthened my resolve, giving me the additional courage I desperately needed.

There were only five people in the audience that day, but they listened intently as I talked about human rights abuses, the plight of orphans in Cambodia, and the immense number of people maimed and killed by land mines on a daily basis. My college speech classes had somewhat prepared me for public speaking, but I was still new to it. I relied on my conviction and spoke from my heart. The audience was very kind, and despite my youth and inexperience, they recognized in me a genuine desire to help. The people of Fresno became my true friends and loyal supporters. I was invited back to speak to a group of twenty people and then to a group of five hundred. It wasn't long before I was headed to the California state capitol, Sacramento.

A White Rose

Soon my work with PUAA had consumed me so completely that I had no time to run the donut stores. Phal Kam took over the management, but it was a disaster; he had no idea what he was doing and had no understanding of business matters at all. The stores began to lose money, leaving us in dire straights. He had various girlfriends and squandered whatever profits we managed to make on them. Eventually, we had to sell both stores and with nowhere to live, Mr. Simpson offered to rent space to us in his apartment building. At the time, he was living in a building on Alamitos Avenue, in a nice part of Long Beach. The apartment complex was two stories tall, painted bright white with wrought iron grills over the windows, and had several beds of bright flowers surrounding it. Mr. Simpson lived in apartment eight on the second floor and Phal Kam, Reachiny and I moved in below him into apartment four. An external staircase ran between the two floors.

Every morning, I would go up to his apartment and cook breakfast for him—the spicy rice and fish soup that he loved so much. It gave us a chance to talk and for me to continue learning the ways of politics. Mr. Simpson allowed us to live rent-free in the apartment for almost two years while I continued my work with PUAA and while my so-called "marriage" to Phal Kam fell apart.

In January of 1999, I made Mr. Simpson breakfast as usual, but that day he surprised me with the gift of a single white rose and began talking about how much he loved roses. To him, he said, they represented the fragile beauty of life. The tone in his voice disturbed me. He spoke like someone who was about to leave, and as I left, I felt that he knew something I did not. Shortly thereafter, he called me back into his apartment and began making a list of all the things that he would like me to accomplish, acting as though he would not be around to see our plans come to fruition. His mood was quite morose as he said, "You know, Oni, my spirit will remain with you after I am gone." It was obvious that he expected to die soon, and I was frightened at the prospect of losing him.

Soon after Mr. Simpson had given me the rose, Reachiny fell ill with a cold. She cried wretchedly and was miserable. It was a Saturday afternoon, and we were upstairs visiting Mr. Simpson. He offered to fetch her some ice cream, hoping that it would soothe her sore throat. Reachiny stayed in his apartment waiting for her treat while I went back downstairs to finish some work. Reachiny returned home later that evening, but she returned in a state of extreme agitation.

"There's a ghost in the bathroom," she said. "I don't want to go in there."

The next day she complained of the ghost again, this time saying she saw it in the entrance hall of the building. Nothing I said could comfort her, and I had never seen my daughter so terrified.

I did not see Mr. Simpson at all the following day. I spent most of the day trying to comfort Reachiny. On Monday morning, the phone rang while I was cleaning our apartment. It was Mr. Simpson's son-in-law, Allen, asking if I knew where Mr. Simpson was. It seemed that he had missed a court appearance scheduled for nine o'clock that morning, which was worrisome since he was an extremely punctual person. I was afraid of what I might find if I went to Mr. Simpson's apartment on my own, especially since I had a feeling that something was wrong. I called Mr. Simpson's friend, and together we went upstairs to his apartment. We found my dear mentor lying face down on the parquet floor, just inside the room he used as a home office. He died of a heart attack, most likely on the previous Saturday evening. Reachiny and I had been the last people to see him alive. He passed away on January 11, 1999, and his funeral was a bittersweet experience. Although I had suffered the deaths of many close friends in my short life, this was the first time I had the opportunity to formally say goodbye at a service. The service certainly helped sooth my nerves and had a calming effect on my soul, but it did not change the fact that, once again, I had lost a very dear guardian.

Mr. Simpson filled many roles in my life; he guided me, educated me, and transformed me. Without him, I would never have known how to even begin my work for the Cambodian community. He gave me the political skills I needed, provided me with contacts, and shoved me forward when I hesitated or was unsure of myself. He taught me how to believe in myself and follow my dreams; he helped me to build my self-esteem while reminding me to always remain humble. He showed me the value and wisdom of learning to crawl before you walk, of never giving up when you have something valuable to contribute, of always being fair, of always maintaining a positive and happy attitude, and of the importance of using caution when exercising power. He believed in honesty, goodness, and helping others. He expected the same things from me.

Sadly, he never had the chance to visit Cambodia. We always promised each other that one day we would visit Angkor Wat together, but it was not to be. Still, when I finally return there, I will take Mr. Simpson with me in my heart so that his spirit can enjoy the ancient heart of Cambodia. I will do my utmost to honor his dream of returning peace to my country.

CHAPTER NINETEEN

New Beginnings

The months following Mr. Simpson's death were difficult, and stunned by his absence, I was barely able to function. Without his assistance, we were unable to pay rent on the apartment to the new owner. Phal Kam and I separated, and Reachiny and I moved in with a friend, Marin Nhean Has, who lived on Freeman Avenue.

I found peace in Marin's home. She fed us, clothed us, and lavished us with love and support. Suddenly, I had a mother again, and Reachiny discovered the pleasures of having a grandmother. We settled into family life with a great sense of relief. Gradually my heart settled down, began to heal, and I was able to bring focus and organization back into my life. Marin's lifestyle was wholly uncomplicated and at the same time filled with a simple beauty that I cherished. She was a skilled seamstress and supported herself by making and selling beautiful Cambodian wedding dresses. Her creations were inspired by the classic designs from the royal court of Cambodia, and I enjoyed being able to help her sew dresses in return for my share of the rent; it was an arrangement that suited us both. After working at PUAA all day, I spent the evenings sewing dresses with Marin. We generally used this time to talk about our days, but sometimes we sat in silence, simply basking in the comfort of each other's presence.

I had come full circle. I was once again sitting in an apartment, sewing clothes as I had done when I lived with Mrs. Touch. Yet the circumstances here were so vastly different. Back then, I felt like a slave. With Marin, I was free and I sewed because I chose to.

At first, I did not tell Marin anything particular about my background. She knew I was a refugee like herself, but knew nothing of my lineage until one evening when we got to talking about our pasts.

It turned out that Marin's father had been an officer in the Cambodian army and had worked with my father. It was one of those wonderful instances of serendipity that reminds one of God's infinitely mysterious ways. In my new American life, I drew strength from the roots of my history, which extended through the center of the world and transcended time. Now, through Marin, I had once again connected with my parents and the life I had lived in Cambodia.

On September 19, 1999, with the help and support of my friends in Fresno, Long Beach, and Sacramento, and with the silent support of Mr. Simpson that I carried in my heart, PUAA, The Foundation for Cambodia was officially registered as a non-profit corporation in the state of California. Over three hundred people attended the inaugural celebration, and it was a great day for my friends, my supporters, and me. While I realized that there were still difficult times ahead and that the path I had chosen would not be an easy one, I knew that my life had definitely turned a corner. Finally, I could see a shimmer of light on the horizon. The pain and suffering, the losses, the disappointments, the abuse and opposition all seemed to be receding. I had somewhere to go and a family to support me in that journey. I was emerging from a long, dark tunnel, and for the first time, I was stepping out into the light.

In the ten years since its official incorporation, PUAA has continued to grow in both strength and influence. A core group of dedicated individuals gathers in our offices daily, selflessly devoting themselves to fulfilling the organization's goals. Mr. Simpson's strategy of letter writing has proven to be extremely effective. Gradually, one letter at a time, our cause is being recognized. People and organizations throughout the world have begun to take notice of our vision, and many have joined our cause. Recent movies filmed at Angkor Wat, such as Tomb Raider, have brought international awareness to the beauty of our culture, as well as to the plight of our citizens. Celebrities such as Angelina Jolie, Matt Damon, and Danny Glover have been inspired to lend their names to Cambodian causes. In America, the Cambodian community is one of the emerging immigrant population groups whose votes are eagerly sought by politicians belonging to both parties in state and national elections alike. Republicans and Democrats have actively sought PUAA's help in reaching Cambodian voters in California.

In recent years, as a representative of PUAA, I received invitations to Capitol Hill, and I attended the inauguration ceremony of President George W. Bush. I lobbied the United States Congress to hold accountable those who were behind the Khmer Rouge Genocide. It is frustrating when our voices are heard, yet ignored, but we keep our focus on the children who will benefit from our unceasing action. I speak regularly with people at the United Nations, the American Red Cross, and various other humanitarian organizations, and I often receive invitations to celebrity fundraisers. PUAA, The Foundation for Cambodia, has established links with many other organizations such as the Australian Aid for Cambodia Foundation (AACF), an Australian foundation that sponsors schools in rural Cambodia. In February of 2002, PUAA received a license to operate in Cambodia and now operates a service center in Phnom Penh, giving us the chance to implement some of our programs in Cambodia itself. Much work lies ahead of us, but the doors seem to be opening, and the future is bright and optimistic. Our cause draws people from all backgrounds and all nationalities, and for the first time in my life, I do not feel alone.

I plan to return to Cambodia soon, after an absence of almost twenty years. I was eleven years old when, as a frightened but determined young child, I escaped with the hope of finding a better life in America. Although I arrived in the U.S. with an adopted family, I was truly alone, and I remained alone for quite a while. When I return to Cambodia, it will be with my daughter at my side and a whole team of PUAA members for support. I am apprehensive and frightened of this journey, but I know that this time I will not have to face the history I share with so many other Cambodians on my own.

I do not know what challenges and opportunities I will face there. When it is the right time to go back, I will trust in God to protect me on my mission. I hope to eventually complete Lork Ta Sar's charge of bringing peace back to Cambodia; I know that the process began as soon as I found peace in my own heart. No country has suffered like Cambodia, and no other country is more deserving of a safe and peaceful future. It has the tradition and the heart to accomplish great things. It has peace deep in the soul of its people, it has the desire, and perhaps it has the destiny. Only time can tell, but when I do put my foot on Cambodian soil again, I hope it will be the first step in a journey towards peace and that many will join us in our efforts.

Reflections

Why God tests his children the way he does can be hard to understand until one reflects back upon it. When I look back at the experiences in my life so far, I am both amazed and humbled. I am amazed that any human being could have experienced so much pain, so much death, and so much destruction, especially as a child, and I am humbled by the power inherently present in those who survive and overcome such trials. My life was hard, it was terrifying, and at times, it seemed hopeless, but without all those obstacles, without all that suffering, I would not be the woman I am today. I am proud to be this woman, and I carry inside me the strength of an entire nation.

I have looked in the face of death on more occasions than I can remember. I have witnessed people killed by bullets and bombs, beaten with sticks, smashed by hoes, humiliated and degraded. I have seen women raped and abused and young children slaughtered. I have stood on the edge of burial pits waiting for the final blow to fall that would consign me to an eternity spent rotting in an anonymous grave. I have lived in fear and desperation and eaten rats and garbage in order to stay alive. I have been cold and alone without a glimmer of hope. I have lost parents, friends, and loved ones, suffered beatings and abuse. I have tried to end my life more than once, but been fortunate enough to fail each time. It seems that there is nothing horrible in the world that I have not experienced.

The most important lesson I learned throughout all the hardships I faced is this: You always have a choice in how you deal with the aftermath of an experience. You can become overwhelmed, sink into despair, and allow yourself to live life as a victim, or you can rise above the pain and consciously take your life to a higher level.

There is a Cambodian story about a master who grew tired of his apprentice continually complaining about his own unhappiness. So one day he sent his apprentice to fetch some salt. When the apprentice returned, the master instructed the unhappy young man to put a handful of the salt in a glass of water and then drink it.

"How does it taste?" the master asked.

"Bitter," said the apprentice as he gagged on the saltwater.

The master chuckled and then asked the young man to take the same handful of salt and put it in the nearby lake. The disciple did so, and as instructed, swirled the water around with his hand to thoroughly mix the salt.

"Now drink from the lake," instructed the wise old man. "How does it taste?" he asked as the water dripped from the young man's chin.

"Fresh," replied the apprentice.

"Do you taste the salt?" asked the master.

"No," said the young man.

The master sat down beside his apprentice and offered the following words of wisdom: "The pain of life is pure salt. No more, no less. The amount of pain in life remains exactly the same. However, the amount of bitterness we taste depends on the container we put the pain in. So when you are in pain, the only thing you can do is to enlarge your sense of things. Stop being a glass, become a lake."

When you survive traumatic events, you gain great power over them. Fear and emotional pain are never as powerful once you have faced them. Even the most difficult and painful experiences have something to teach us. As Lork Ta Sar predicted, in order to understand the suffering of my people, I had to suffer myself. When I write to the High Commission on Human Rights about abuses in Cambodia, I am able to utilize details from my own experience. When I appeal to the President of the United States about child abuse in Cambodia, I am describing what I have seen and felt. When I appeal to the United Nations about the dangers of land mines in my country, it is because I have witnessed the awful damage they do to innocent people. When I bring attention to the necessity of schools for children in Cambodia, it is because I know what it is like to struggle through life without a proper education. Everything that occurred in my life gives me power in the form of passion—passion to remove these evils from the world, passion to fight for freedom and justice, passion for developing a democratic government, passion for equality and passion to eliminate poverty, not just in Cambodia, but for all people in the world, and especially the children who will inhabit the world that we create and bequeath to them.

We cannot change the past, but we can alter the course of the future. With each moment we have the ability to make a choice that will counteract the effects of our previous actions. If you want to change the future in a positive direction, start doing positive things for others today.

In my short life I have learned so much about the human condition. All of us have a tendency to judge people as good or bad. I believe we cannot readily dismiss any person as completely evil or reject any human being as unredeemable. I do not mean this in any particular religious sense. I mean it in a universal sense, equally applicable to all human beings from all religions, cultures, races or governments. The reality is that we each have to work on improving ourselves, and we each have to help others improve themselves. We are not separate human beings living in isolation. The life of an African villager is not irrelevant to the life of a New Yorker and the atrocities in Cambodia are not unimportant to a farmer in Iowa. Each atrocity committed is a blow to every human being in the world as we are all part of a world family and we are all connected. Each time someone suffers, we all will suffer on some level. If we want peace in the world for ourselves, we have to create peace for everyone.

There is a theory in physics called the Chaos Theory that describes how truly interconnected everything is. The theory states that when a butterfly flaps its wings in Japan, the minute physical disturbance in the atmosphere can cause a chain of reaction that can, theoretically, lead to a hurricane on the other side of the world. If such a delicate action can create such a dramatic result, what are the consequences for the rest of humanity when any human being, especially a child, suffers or dies in pain?

We cannot force change in another person, nor can we force them to do what we want them to do. Our primary focus must be on changing ourselves. As Jesus said, we must first remove the plank from our own eye before we remove the speck of dust from another's. We must lead by example, and we must help others who are less fortunate than we are. We must do this with compassion in our hearts and forgiveness in our souls. Education is vital in this process as knowledge is a powerful force to fight suffering. Generosity is required as no man is truly wealthy while another is poor. Fairness and justice must always be utilized, but not without wisdom and benevolence, for it is better to rehabilitate a man than discard or reject him. Above all, we must love one another and cherish the existence of every man, woman, and child.

PART TWO

Short History Of Cambodia

Much of the early history of Cambodia has been lost and what remains exists only in stories passed down from generation to generation. Perhaps the earliest of these stories describes Cambodia as originally being an island with only one tree. This place was called Kokthlork, or Place for Enlightenment and Peace, a Khmer Garden of Eden.

According to another legend recorded by the Chinese scholar K'Ang T'ai in the 3rd century A.D., the present kingdom of the Khmers has its origins approximately 2000 years ago. The legend says that the vessel of an Indian prince named Kaundinya was blown offshore and landed at the mouth of what is now the Mekong Delta in a land then known to the Chinese as Funan. (This may be a derivation of the Khmer name Phnom, meaning mountain.) The ship may have been in search of the fabled Suvarnabhumi, or land of gold, a popular diversion among Indian seafarers of the time. The prince apparently had a dream in which his favorite god blessed him with a magical bow and instructed him to set sail overseas. At dawn, when he went to pray in the temple, he discovered the bow from his dream. Inspired by this divine event, the prince decided to embark on his voyage. Once at sea, however, the god changed the course of the winds so that the vessel was forced to land in Funan, thereby setting in motion the chain of events that led to the founding of the Khmer dynasty.

Once in Funan, the vessel was attacked by local soldiers led by their queen, Lieu-Ye, or Willowleaf, who was in the habit of preying on seafarers blown astray and onto the shores of her territory. Kaundinya, however, subdued the queen with his divine bow and took Willowleaf as his prisoner. When captured, she was completely naked as was the tradition in her land, a fact that proved very embarrassing to the Indian prince who immediately had her wrapped in a sari to cover her nakedness. They later married and from their union were born the Khmer race.

Early accounts of the state of Funan and the Khmer people are not very clear, and much has been lost in the mists of time. Still it is obvious from the numerous legends and traditions that this new civilization, the one that would eventually become present day Cambodia, was heavily influenced by the ancient Vedic civilization of India, which had existed on the Indian sub-continent for thousands of years. Over time, large numbers of Indian merchants and travelers, attracted by the rich resources of the Mekong Delta, moved to Funan and married local women bringing with them their beliefs and traditions. The religious and spiritual practices of India, first Hinduism and later Theravada Buddhism, the languages of Sanskrit and Pali, temple rituals, astronomy, and the legal system all seem to have been imported from India.

Despite conflicts with other principalities in the region, Funan apparently prospered. An early account by Chinese historians described it as having " . . . walled towns, palaces, and houses. The people mostly take their food on silver utensils. The taxes are paid in gold, silver, pearls, and perfumes. They have many books. In writing, they use an alphabet derived from India."

By the 9th century A.D., The Khmer civilization under the rule of the devaraja, or god-king, Jayavarman II, emerged as a dominant power in the region. The king established an empire that eventually stretched from the Gulf of Tonkin in present-day Vietnam in the east, to the west coast of present-day Thailand. This was the golden age of the Khmer people. The king was revered as a representative of the divine rule of their gods. In the Vedic tradition, the king is part of the solar dynasty and rules his earthly kingdom in the same way that the sun rules the heavens. The cosmic intelligence of creation, they believed, could be harnessed to rule the temporal kingdom on earth. Under Jayavarman's patronage, Brahmin priests performed traditional Vedic ceremonies, yagyas and pandits, to ensure that life was kept in tune with divine law so that peace, prosperity, and harmony with the environment were maintained. In the Vedic tradition, the gods were honored as the living embodiment of cosmic intelligence who managed the different aspects of creation. By paying proper attention to these divinities, success in life was assured.

For the next 600 hundred years the Khmer civilization flourished. Jayavarman II and his successors presided benevolently over a rich, fertile, and prosperous land. Nature was abundant in her gifts and blessed them with up to four rice crops a year. Unlimited supplies of fish were available from the huge Tonle Sap Lake, set like a jewel in the heart of their empire. Culture, the arts, and learning flourished. Their armies were invincible, keeping at bay the forces of the Chams (present-day Vietnamese) on the east and the Siamese (present-day Thai) on the west.

To pay homage to the gods, who they believed were their source of power, the kings launched a temple-building program of a size rarely seen in history, comparable in its magnificence to the ancient pyramids of Egypt or the imposing Aztec and Mayan structures of Central America. Expert Brahmin architects were brought in from India to make sure that the temples were built according to the proper cosmic proportions, a science known in the Vedic tradition as Sthapatya Veda. They believed that political and spiritual power combined in these awe-inspiring edifices that were designed to ensure continued divine blessings from the gods and support from the natural elements. For a society so dependant on its agricultural production, it was especially important that the seasons arrived on time, that the land was fertile, and that the rains were plentiful and so these temples were designed to please the gods. During one forty-year period in the reign of King Jayavarman VII alone (1181–1219), twelve massive temple complexes were completed.

The most famous of these temple structures, Angkor Wat, was built in the 12th century under King Suryavarman II, a devoted follower of Vishnu, the Vedic deity believed responsible for creation and preservation. It was built as a home for all the gods of the Vedic pantheon with Vishnu reigning supreme, his image facing in all four cardinal directions. The central tower represented Mount Meru, the home of the gods in heaven and the moats that surrounded the temple city were the ocean of milk on which Vishnu traditionally resides. In the Vedic tradition, when a statue to a god is properly sculpted and installed, it is believed that the spirit of the deity literally enters it and the statue becomes a living entity, not just a piece of carved stone. To the Khmer people of that time, Angkor Wat was a living, breathing celestial city. At its height of success in the 12th century, the population of this divinely inspired city may have reached as much as one million residents. At the same time, Paris, one of the greatest cities of Europe had no more than thirty thousand citizens.

The walls of Angkor Wat were adorned with bas-relief sculptures of Vedic gods and Sanskrit carvings of Vedic literature. The entire epic of the Ramayana, the life story of the Indian god-king Rama and his triumph over the evil demon Ravanna, was depicted in one huge section of the complex. Vivid battle scenes of the Khmer heroes defending their kingdom against the invading Cham and Siamese armies were also portrayed. When Angkor Wat was finally released from its jungle captivity less than 70 years ago, a rich heritage of Khmer civilization was discovered in the Sanskrit, Pali, and Khmer inscriptions that covered the walls.

In 1431, after a series of relentless raids, Thai armies finally laid siege to Angkor Wat and the Khmer rulers withdrew to establish their capital in the region of present day Phnom Penh. No one knows for sure why this happened.

The next 500 years of Khmer history is very unclear. What is known is that by the middle of the 15th century, the Khmer nation was subject to Thai rule and that for most of the 18th century and well into the 19th century, the Thai and the Vietnamese fought for control of the region. Angkor Wat itself fell into obscurity until it was discovered completely overgrown with jungle by Cambodian explorers in the 1860s.

In the middle of the 19th century, the Cambodian king, Ang Dong, with his country imposed upon by two powerful neighbors, Thailand and Vietnam, requested help from the French. Napoleon III responded eagerly, demanding numerous trading privileges in return for using French military power to defend the country. In 1863, Cambodia officially became a French protectorate. In true colonial fashion, France then proceeded to increase its influence over Cambodia, as well as Thailand and Vietnam.

Although the Cambodian court was prepared to live with the French influence in return for its independence from Thai rule (granted in 1907) and protection from Vietnamese designs on its territory, the majority of the population suffered from an oppressive colonial regime, which brought with it an excessive tax burden. The boiling point came in 1925, when an abusive French tax official and his staff were murdered in the Kompong Chhnang Province. Anti-colonial sentiments began to spread among the Cambodian intelligentsia. Nationalist leaders such as Pach Chhoeun, Son Ngoc, and Sim Var succeeded in launching the first Cambodian newspaper in 1935, *Ngara Vatta,* and used it to voice anti-colonial opinions. When Japanese forces took over the country in 1941, the anti-colonialists were given a chance to speak out against their French masters, an opportunity they took full advantage of.

In April of the same year, the French appointed western-educated Norodom Sihanouk as the new king-in-exile, assuming of course, that he would support their continuing rule when he returned to the country. However, when the French regained Cambodia from the defeated Japanese forces at the end of World War II, Sihanouk surprised them by becoming a champion for Cambodia's sovereignty.

Yet while the king worked for independence, thirty-seven thousand Cambodians, including the cadre's leaders, were slaughtered in a Vietnamese resistance trap. In 1947–1948, the Vietminh (Vietnamese organizations for the Liberation of Vietnam based in Kampuchea Krom) proposed to their Cambodian colleagues a meeting to discuss the possibility of working together to liberate the country from the colonial power of France. Both sides agreed on the agenda, date, and location. The Vietminh also requested that the Cambodians bring no arms in order to avoid the suspicion of the French soldiers and because it was to be an intellectual meeting between international leaders.

The Cambodians of Kampuchea Krom arrived at the granges, which were the appointed meeting place. After a few moments of pleasantries, the Vietnamese slipped out the door, escaping to the outside; they locked the Cambodians inside the grange door and then torched the structure. Thirty-seven thousand Khmer from Kampuchea Krom were burned alive in the grange within the space of a few hours. These people were Cambodia's teachers, leaders, and deacons. Very few were able to escape the fire and return to Cambodia. The Vietnamese awaited Cambodia's reaction, knowing that it would be brutal and savage.

The French government sided with Vietnamese leaders, and French colonial authorities soon dismissed all Cambodians appointed to the ranks of Vice-Mayor and Vice-Governor. The French and Vietnamese leaders wrote new constitutional laws for Cambodia. They entrusted all Kampuchea Krom leadership to the Vietnamese, even though the vast majority of the population was Cambodian. The administration and the praetorian guards were now under Vietnamese leadership.

In 1953, after visiting the United States, France, Japan, and Canada to plead his cause, King Sihanouk declared a royal crusade for independence for his country. The French, already embroiled in a war in Vietnam, were too weak to resist, and in November of that year granted Cambodians their independence. Sihanouk had succeeded in releasing Cambodia from its colonial masters with a nonviolent campaign reminiscent of those crusades led by Mahatma Gandhi.

Inspired by his previous success, King Sihanouk plunged into reorganizing the country, abdicating the throne in favor of his father so he could focus on political and social reform. At first this move proved to be very successful—farmers reaped bumper harvests and the establishment of industry and commerce began. However, crucial mistakes were made in foreign policy that threw Cambodia unsuspectingly into the middle of the Cold War and set the country on a collision course with the United States, who was now actively involved in fighting communist forces in Vietnam.

Sihanouk openly supported the forces of Ho Chi Minh in their fight against the Americans in North Vietnam, allowing the Vietminh soldiers to secretly travel inside Cambodia down what became known as the Ho Chi Minh Trail, which was, in fact, a series of trails through Laotian and Cambodian territory. This policy alienated the American government at a crucial time when other Cambodian politicians were seeking closer ties. In 1961 and 1963, Sihanouk severed diplomatic ties with Thailand and North Vietnam—two of America's closest Asian allies—further aggravating relations with the United States. Shortly afterwards, Sihanouk cut off all American aid and launched strong anti-American editorials in the Cambodian press, which he controlled in an attempt to establish Cambodian neutrality in the Southeast Asian conflict. The lack of American financing and support was devastating to the Cambodian economy, sending the country into a downward spiral. The growing political gulf between the nations was disastrously widened. Cambodia was left alone and weak in the midst of one of the most violent regional conflicts of the century.

It is possible that then United States President John F. Kennedy would have worked to restore the situation. He proposed a three hundred and fifty million dollar contribution to aid Cambodia. However, Sihanouk, then ruler of Cambodia, was highly concerned about the power the American government could have over him. Unfortunately, the assassination of President Kennedy occurred before his administration had even left for Cambodia. His administration never had the opportunity to see King Sihanouk and convince him to change his mind and accept U.S. aid. Sihanouk broke off discussions with the United States and allied himself with North Vietnam. He planned to reject the United States and turn instead to China and France. Unfortunately, France and China were unable to replace the aid promised by America, and the Cambodian people suffered for it. Cambodia plunged into an economic recession, aggravated by the erosion of an overlong rule and political corruption.

The untimely death of President Kennedy in November of 1963 ended any attempt by the United States to heal relations with Cambodia. By 1964, U.S. forces began to attack Cambodian territory, and in May 1965, they severed any remaining diplomatic relations. By 1969, the United States had begun secret air raids on suspected Vietnamese hideouts in Cambodia, and American bombs were claiming the lives of thousands of innocent civilians. It was the victory of the North Vietnamese armed forces at the battle of Dien Bien Phu against the French colonial powers that led to the 1954 Geneva Peace Agreement of Indochina. The Geneva Peace Agreement stipulated that all armed forces had to withdraw from Cambodian territory. North Vietnam never respected this clause. Their armed forces infrastructure remained in tact in Cambodia, even after the Geneva Agreement on Cambodia in 1991 reaffirmed this clause, stating that all foreign troops should withdraw.

Vietnam never respected or followed the Geneva Agreement of 1954, nor did they respect the agreement between the United States and North Vietnam in Paris of 1973 (the Kissinger and Le Duc Tho negotiation), nor their Paris Agreements of 1991. Instead, the Vietnamese installed themselves in all levels of the Khmer Rouge armed forces fighting against the Lon Nol pro-occident regime and were able to reach high-ranking levels of power during this time of conflict.

It was very hard for Cambodia to secure armed forces independent from Vietnam, especially while the United States supported French colonialism. North Vietnamese control of Cambodia was all encompassing. The country was under the thumb of Vietnam, and when Cambodia finally manifested its independence, the Vietminh answered with a threat of assassination of the Cambodian people.

In January of 1970, Sihanouk left for France to take his annual holiday. While he was away, his opponents mobilized to overthrow him. On March 18, disenchanted army officers captured Prime Minister Lon Nol at gunpoint and forced him to support a motion in the national assembly to remove Sihanouk. The next day, by a vote of 86–3, Sihanouk was ejected from office. Lon Nol remained Prime Minister and the new republican government won immediate recognition and financial support from America. Sihanouk found himself in exile and sought asylum in communist China.

While all this was going on, a communist movement had been gaining ground in the rural areas. The movement was originally a genuine attempt to improve living conditions for the poor people of Cambodia by setting up a strong agrarian economy. In the background, however, were the unseen hands of the Chinese and North Vietnamese communist governments, who both coveted the rich resources of the Cambodian countryside.

The leader of the rising communist movement was a young man known as Salot Sar. Sar later changed his name to Pol Pot (meaning population of politics). While a student in Paris, where it seems he ignored his studies to become an active member of the Communist Party, he had already incurred the wrath of Sihanouk by calling for the elimination of the monarchy. He returned to Cambodia in 1953 to take charge of the emerging Khmer People's Revolutionary Party. The party's chief targets were the French colonials, the growing American presence in the region, and Sihanouk himself who labeled them the "Khmer Rouge" and tried to suppress them by force. By the time Sihanouk was removed from office in 1970, however, Pol Pot and his Khmer Rouge had spread their brand of Maoist class struggle and agrarian reform throughout much of the Cambodian countryside.

In a bizarre turn of events, Sihanouk then allied himself with Pol Pot, urging him to overthrow the new government of Lon Nol and reinstate him as leader. Hun Sen was then a student in Phnom Penh and a loyal supporter of Sihanouk. Responding to Sihanouk's call, Hun Sen quit his studies and fled to the jungle to join the Khmer Rouge. As the Khmer Rouge armies gained the upper hand and advanced on the capital city of Phnom Penh, the U.S. Embassy was shut down on April 12, 1975. Five days later, King Sihanouk turned Cambodia's capital into a ghost town as it fell to the Khmer Rouge and the years of slaughter and oppression began.

Pol Pot permitted Sihanouk to return to the capital later that year, but he was kept a virtual prisoner in the royal palace unaware of the atrocities that his supposed friends were committing around the country. Under the guise of a pending American attack, the entire city of Phnom Penh was evacuated and several million inhabitants were condemned to a life on the road and in rural work camps. The capital city became a mere husk of its former glory, money was banned, educated and professional people were chased down and murdered, and the entire country was turned into a concentration camp where fear, hardship, and death became the dominant conditions. What began as an agrarian revolution turned into a genocidal campaign. It is estimated that 3.5 million innocent Cambodians were tortured, starved and beaten to death in a four-year period, but the actual figure may well be much higher.

International horror at the events in Cambodia eventually lead to the overthrow of Pol Pot and the Khmer Rouge in 1979 by Vietnamese forces who were strengthened by their recent victory over the Americans. They established a new government under the leadership of the young Hun Sen. As Prime Minister, Hun Sen has proven to be a very durable leader, but his administration is riddled with scandalous corruption.

There is currently no real legal system that protects the poor and innocent Khmer people—there is only a legal system that the rich and affluent are immune to. A large majority, 85% of the Khmer population, are living in absolute poverty, barely able to survive in the countryside.

Ex-King Sihanouk retired and asked the Hun Sen-led government to elect Prince Sihamoni as the new king of Cambodia. He was named king on October 14, 2004. The Khmer people hope he will be the first king to highlight a strong foundation of a free society, and that he will help to enact changes in the structure of the country's laws.

Cambodia is currently in bad condition and its future as a society is bleak. Years of war have depleted the country and left it exhausted, and as a result, it ranks among the poorest countries in the world. A strong economic infrastructure is not yet in place, and the education system, a critical component for economic recovery, is struggling to reestablish itself. The corruption among government officials contributes to the delay in progress. Thailand and Vietnam, both historic rivals for dominance in the region, are much stronger and create pressure from both the East and the West, while to the North, China remains a threat as it enviously looks upon the rich agricultural land of Cambodia as a source of food for its constantly expanding population.

Fortunately, Cambodia has a rich cultural and political heritage and the country is plentiful in natural resources. Though still reeling from the years of war and slaughter, deep inside there is a resilient spirit and the will to survive and grow strong again.

A Personal Experience by Michael Blasdell, Country Development Director, PUAA, The Foundation for Cambodia

At first, the image confused me because I was unsure of what I was looking at. The photograph lay upside down on a counter among many other images that a clerk had laid out in a photo shop in Saigon, Vietnam, where I had been living for three years. The clerk picked up the photo, and as it moved through the air, my vision focused on it and the edges of the room seemed to fade away. In my mind, I stood quietly and observed the clerk's actions, but at the same time, I heard my voice asking to see the picture. Suddenly, the photograph appeared in front of me and as I gazed upon the Temple for the first time, I was awestruck, barely able to believe that I had never before seen a picture of this place. A surge of feeling overcame me as I looked at the image that was both strange and calming. It was as though a long-lost friend had suddenly crossed my path in an unexpected place, and although I felt in my heart that I recognized the form, I couldn't quite make sense of why it was so familiar.

I felt a consuming need to learn more about this picture and asked the clerk. She told me that it was Angkor Wat, the most grand of many temples in a very ancient complex located in the jungles of Cambodia. The pictures were like nothing I had ever seen, and as I continued to look at the other photographs, I vaguely remembered an image I had seen years ago. It was a mystical face carved out of stone with jungle roots intertwining its blocks, giving it an ethereal presence. At that moment, I decided that if this complex was home to that face, I had to walk among the ruins. I had no idea how to make that happen, especially when I heard it was in Cambodia. I felt intensely disappointed. I was far too busy at the time to make such a long journey, and the deadly Khmer Rouge soldiers continued to actively wage battles in that country.

I have long since learned that the powers that be have ways to ensure that the unknowing fulfill their destinies. A few weeks later I met with representatives of the Royal Kingdom of Cambodia, and it was their wish that I travel with them to Phnom Penh. I agreed to the trip, and after the meetings concluded, I mentioned that I desired to visit Angkor Wat. The representatives voiced their concerns that travel was too dangerous; the night belonged to the Khmer Rouge. They also reminded me of our recent drive up from Saigon during which the entire length of the main road was heavily guarded by troops and a second vehicle with armed guards always followed us. It was true that I had seen more than just a few armored vehicles on the roads, and I knew the fields were saturated with land mines (which made for some interesting rest stops, as no one was willing to step even one yard off the main road to relieve themselves). Even when I traveled around Phnom Penh, we had AK-47 machine guns in our cars and two plain-clothed military guards in tow. The more they attempted to persuade me not to go, the more it seemed to me that it was not a matter for them to decide. I was halfway around the world from my home, and I realized I might never have this chance again, so this visit needed to happen then.

Along with some guards, I booked a flight to Siem Reap, Cambodia, and upon landing, rented a car and headed out on a small, bumpy dirt road. The scenery along the road was dotted with houses that were merely bamboo huts with walls and roofs crafted of palm fronds. The only traffic was comprised of locals on bicycles who carried firewood and water. I gazed at the horizon through the windshield when suddenly, between the green leaves of the jungle, a large stone tower appeared in the distance. I immediately called for the car to stop. I got out, stood in the road and confirmed what I saw. I felt excitement about what was revealed among the trees ahead, and I took a photograph to memorialize that moment when I first saw the temple.

We came to the end of the road, and I felt my stomach tingle as one of the most beautiful sights I had ever seen came into view. For there, rising above the red dust cloud we traveled in, were lotus bud-shaped towers that seemed to float in the clear blue sky. As the dust settled, the full magnificence of the temple became clear, and the majestic spires that towered over large galleries of hallways revealed themselves. I immediately experienced a sense of wonder, as the size of the complex became apparent; we were still more than a mile away.

We parked the car and stepped onto the huge, elevated causeway by which we could enter the outer gallery of the temple. Orange-colored stones with fearsomely carved lions positioned to frighten all that attempted to pass stood out in bold contrast to the vast expanse of pink lotus flowers that flourished on the carpet of green platter-shaped leaves in the moat that surrounded the temple. On either side of us, the tea-colored water smelled of humid vegetation and the massive stone paving at my feet made me feel as though I was entering the home of ancient giants.

The presence of the temple called to me, and as I went through the main entrance, I felt like I was coming home. Initially, my attention was drawn to the long hallways that ran to the sides where carvings were painstakingly etched into the walls. Then I caught a glimpse of something amazing, framed in the stone doorway before me. I cannot imagine a more perfectly beautiful sight than my first glimpses of the Angkor Wat temple through that door. For there, brightly lit by the early morning sun, standing magnificently at the end of a second grand stone causeway, was truly one of the last existing wonders of the world. In all my memories of traveling, I could not recall any other image being so awe-inspiring.

The inner courtyard's deep green grass and blue, reflective pools accented the main temple's awesome presence. Banisters along the causeway, carved into the shape of the great snake god, Naga, beckoned me onward. At each landing, Naga reared up with seven heads full of menacing teeth to warn against evil trespassers.

Buddhist monks in ocher robes chanted their early morning prayers in the galleries, and bells chimed in the distance. Upon reaching the entrance of the second gallery, we climbed more stairs that were guarded by four menacing stone lions, and at the end of a hallway was a huge statue of Vishnu with his many arms outstretched as if in welcome. I stood before him and found myself greeting the statue with a small pranam, a bowing of the head with palms together and touching the forehead. In another alcove, a stone Buddha, worn smooth by loving hands, was draped with the brilliant orange fabric of a monk, a candle flickering at its feet. In the Gallery of a Thousand Buddha's, worshippers had assembled statues of all sizes, and there was a tangible silence left by the countless prayers chanted there. Proud Khmer warriors carved in stone protected the entranceways with strange looking clubs, and yet each radiated a feeling of peace. The center of the temple had four Buddha shrines facing the cardinal points of the compass and carvings of apsarases, the celestial dancers who performed for the gods in heaven, serenely smiled at me from every corner and wall. Their bodies and faces were undeniably beautiful, for each dancer had a special lightness of personality given it by its maker.

Monks walked the hallways burning incense in small pots. I wanted the images, the sounds, the smell of the incense, and the cold dampness of the stone to be imbedded in every fiber of my being. The whole history of Khmer civilization was there, carved in stone; the walls were the culture's great storybooks. I walked the circuit of the temple and saw all the great battles, the traditional dances, the ceremonies, the costumes and everyday life recorded for posterity. Doorways had stories carved above them to teach a life lesson to those that passed through, but not all that walked these sacred halls were students of ancient history. These stone storybooks have had new chapters added to them in the last century. There, among the ancient carvings of elephants and gods, were bullet holes that marred walls blackened by fires and covered in sacrilegious graffiti. Angkor Wat suffered terribly during the war years. Its position on high ground in the middle of generally flat terrain made it a strategic military position, and at times, headquarters for Khmer Rouge forces. The surrounding countryside was extensively mined, and even today, the land around Angkor Wat is unsafe for villagers.

As I exited the temple over the great causeway above the lotus ponds, I noticed blast scars in the massive paving rocks left by previous mortar rocket attacks. I stopped, put my hand down to touch the scarred rock, and I imagined the fierce battles that had been fought there. My final thought was that the temple was not protected as it should be.

Thieves and looters continue to pillage the sculptures, encouraged by the escalating price on the international market for Khmer antiquities. Whole walls and friezes have been removed and illegally sold. In the 1980s the Cambodian government removed most of the freestanding sculptures and placed them in storage in nearby Siem Reap. Even then, armed bandits attacked the warehouses and made off with priceless works of art. In many cases, it is difficult to blame these thieves, motivated by hunger; a poor soldier or farmer can feed his family for several years on the money he can get for one piece of sculpture from Angkor Wat. Still, the thriving global market ensures that more than just local peasants are doing the stealing.

We drove toward the Ta Prohm temple, built to honor King Jayavarman VII's mother. Ta Prohm was never restored, so it is still intertwined with and surrounded by nature. We first came upon a causeway with statues of fierce warriors holding tightly to the body of the snake god, Naga. Three-headed elephants flanked these stone warriors and guarded an arched entrance topped by a lotus bud spire carved with four somber faces of Buddha. We continued to a clearing where five machine gun-toting guards stood waiting, for what, I did not want to know. I soon found out that two German tourists were recently killed there, and because we were traveling deeper into the jungle, a few of these guards would be joining us. We walked through another lotus bud-shaped stone gate. On the other side, a long path hacked through the jungle stretched out before us. A surge of adrenaline ran through my body as I realized that I was approaching something cloaked in mystery.

We walked until we came upon a large jumble of rocks. A stone doorway through which we could pass became visible from behind a tree. The rocks were black basalt, covered in green moss and orange lichen and looked as if they had emerged from the sea. Once through the door, I saw a building a short distance away that was enveloped by a massive, octopus-like tree. Lightly colored, serpentine roots spread over and around its doorway, and although the buildings were smaller than Angkor Wat, they were equally magnificent. I heard the sounds of parrots and monkeys in the distance, and I felt as if a tiger might pounce at any moment, its snarling growl warning me to go no further. We entered the ruins and walked on uneven floors through numerous dark hallways that opened up into little alcoves where either lingams or broken statues were displayed. The dampness allowed lichen to grow on most everything, and the huge trees had sent their searching roots into every corner. The high, domed ceilings came alive in a disturbing manner as we passed under scores of bats that slept serenely in the rocky crevices. Their screeches of alarm echoed loudly as we moved onward into the darkness to explore more galleries.

I exited a doorway into an enclosed courtyard that had crisply detailed apsarases smiling coyly at me from every flat surface. Fallen blocks of green and black stone with small plants growing between them added to the look of abandonment about the place. I turned to look at a hauntingly beautiful tree at the far end of the courtyard; it embraced a stone doorway with its roots and it was there and then that it happened. I felt the hair stand up on the back of my neck and a tingling sensation traveled up my spine. There was no doubt in my mind that something was happening and when I reached up to rub my neck, I could feel the hairs bristling. Wondering what caused this reaction, I looked around. My guards were not on alert. In fact, they were doing what many others do in sacred places; they were joking and smoking cigarettes. I started toward the tree, and the closer I came to it, the more pronounced the feeling of energy became. It was a very obvious sensation, and there was a buzzing noise in the atmosphere around me. I stepped over to the guards and asked them to leave me alone for twenty minutes. After they left, I approached the tree again and the energy that returned to my neck and spine was even stronger. This made me step away to take another look at the situation, but since I felt quite as ease with the feeling, I moved forward and positioned my hands on the tree roots coming down from the lintel of the door. I felt a sense of calmness come over me. As I looked up into the heights of the tree, I almost expected to see some jungle spirit sitting up there, watching me.

I could have stayed there forever, but I had to rejoin the real world, and I knew that if something had been awakened inside me, it would stay with me no matter where I went. We concluded our tour by going to the Bayon temple, which stunned me with the complexity of its architecture. I left feeling truly fortunate to have set foot in this marvelous place, deep in the jungles of Cambodia.

Upon my return to the United States, I told my sister, Karen, about my unusual experience in the temple of Ta Prohm, and that I felt my visit to Angkor Wat had changed me somehow. Karen passed on my story to a close friend of hers, Theresa Olson, who was a professor at Maharishi Vedic University in Fairfield, Iowa. Years later, in 2001, she called me and asked if I would help a woman she knew who lived near my home in Long Beach, California.

She explained that this woman, Oni Vitandham, was working on some projects that were sensitive to the Cambodian community and that due to my experience in Cambodia, I should offer her my help. I called Oni and explained to her that I would like to do something to help her cause, but she was cautious of a stranger who called out of the blue. Only after I explained my connection to the professor did she agree to meet and then, only if her Godmother Marin and her seven-year-old daughter could attend. My sister and I had dinner with them, and once I learned what Oni was doing, I offered a cash donation and asked if I could assist her in any other ways. She tersely told me that she did not want my help or my money, but thanked me for my interest in her work. I understood her reluctance to allow a stranger to help her, but who refuses money?

I did not pursue offers of help any further. However, my sister liked Oni very well and they started up a friendship. I often accompanied my sister on her visits with Oni. At this time, my sister was only semi-mobile as she was dying from cancer. I took Karen to Oni's godmother's house and sometimes waited there while they talked. By staying, I was able to get to know Oni's godmother, a well-known seamstress who made beautiful Cambodian clothes. Many Cambodians came to her apartment, and they were a happy group as they spent many hours working, talking, and joking together. They talked about everything from politics to weddings, and I learned a lot about the local Cambodian community, as well as what had happened in their country.

After a few weeks, Karen asked me to do something to help Oni and considering that my sister's health was failing rapidly, I could hardly refuse the request. I approached Oni once more about monetary donations, and again, she refused my offers. I told my sister that it was hopeless to continue offering help, so my sister soon came up with an idea of her own. Marin's apartment was a gathering place for prayer and many Cambodians came there to celebrate religious holidays. Although the apartment was nice enough, it was in obvious need of repainting.

My sister said that Oni could not refuse my help if I donated my time to paint the inside of the apartment, for the gift would benefit many.

Karen explained her plan to Oni, and while we both worked to ease her suspicions, she continued to question us as to why I wanted to help. I explained that I did not know any Cambodians personally, and I believed that if I helped her, she would in turn, be able to help others that I could never reach. With this explanation in mind, she agreed to let me paint the apartment, but she still wanted to know more about me. I showed her my photos of Vietnam and Cambodia, and I described my experiences at the temple. I told her that of all the areas in the world, I felt that Cambodia held something for me, and I just had to find what it was. I mentioned my attachment to Angkor Wat and Ta Prohm, showing her a photo of me standing next to the tree that I felt in my soul was my own. She asked me why I claimed this tree, and I said that I could not explain it, but that I felt that it was true.

After approximately a week, I completed the painting of the apartment and Oni asked if she could speak with me. She asked me to once again tell her about my experiences in the temples, and when I talked about the tree being mine, she interrupted my story and said that I could not have it. I thought she was being playful, so I said, "No, it's my tree."

She said, "No, it was mine first." I then listened to her tell a story from her childhood. Her father had left her with godparents while he went off to fight for Cambodia. When they were killed, she sought shelter first in the Angkor Wat temple and then later in Ta Prohm. My tree was this same tree that she lived under as a small child, and it was there that she first had her vision for the future of Cambodia. I listened to more of her life story, and I felt that if what she was saying was true, the fact that both of us claimed this tree as our own was more than a coincidence.

I soon met the members of the non-profit group that Oni had founded in 1995. I asked the members what it was that they wanted most to accomplish, and they said that their main goal was to establish a system of schools in Cambodia to help the poor. To fulfill my promise to my sister, Karen, I offered to travel to Phnom Penh and arrange for the Kingdom of Cambodia to issue a license for PUAA to operate as an international organization there. In 2001, I signed the license with the

Ministry of Foreign Affairs and the PUAA School became operational. I returned to Angkor Wat and at Ta Prohm, I ran into one of the guards that protected me in 1996. We became good friends, and I would often share meals with his family. I walked with him on his nightly rounds as he guarded the temple, and I greatly enjoyed the profound silence that existed there at midnight. On one clear summer night, the light of a brilliant full moon shone through swaying tree branches and the shadows it cast brought the images of the apsarases dancers to life. I felt immensely fortunate to see them perform, and I wondered what it must have been like to see real dancers, in their fine silk and gold costumes, perform before the king. That night they allowed me to sleep within the temple among the guards, and I awoke at dawn to the sounds of the jungle coming to life.

The next morning, after a small ceremony, I deposited a portion of my departed sister Karen's ashes, along with some ashes of my father and uncle at the base of my tree. Later at the Angkor Wat temple, I deposited more ashes in the innermost section of the central tower that was guarded by a standing Buddha.

The next time I visited Cambodia, it was to set up the new PUAA headquarters in Phnom Penh, and I felt like I was home again. My friend called to tell me that there was a beehive in my tree, and that in the Khmer culture this was deemed a very auspicious event. I was happy to hear this, and even more so the next day when I found a newly made beehive outside my bedroom window. Upon my return to California, I stepped out of my back door and was instantly surrounded by thousands of bees. They circled around me before landing on the wall of my home to build a new hive. In that buzzing cloud, I remembered the words of my friend, and my mind turned to wishes of good things to come for Cambodia.

PHOTOGRAPHS

The ancient temple city of Angkor
reveals Cambodia's rich cultural herit
and second wonder in the world.

Dreaming of peace, justice and hope
for my people to find democracy.

My dear friend and mentor Mr. Robert
Lewis Simpson

President PUAA The Foundation for
Cambodia, David Brooks Arnold, Oni
and Chairman PUAA Foundation for
Cambodia Paul Sweet.

PUAA Country Development Director
Michael Blasdell Audience with the
King Norodom Sihamoni

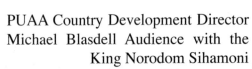

PHOTOGRAPHS

PUAA Country Development Director and Savan Ouch work together to promote strong educational programs in Cambodia.

Philadelphia Chapter of PUAA The Foundation for Cambodia

PUAA Chapter from Long Beach, Fresno, San Francisco, and Stockton, California.

Northern California Chapter of PUAA The Foundation for Cambodia with the Venerable Rev. Savan Chau

Los Angeles County Supervisor Don Knabe
and Oni

Oni with
Senator Dianne Feinstien
in Los Angeles, 1999

Actor Matt Damon, with Susan Cox Giffc
and Oni, attending the premier of
"My Khmer Heart", at the Director's Gui
of America, Hollywood, California.

My daughter Reachiny and
Oni with
Senator Elizabeth Dole
at her Swearing-In Ceremony
January 7, 2003

Actor Danny Glover, my daughter Reachiny, Marissa Castro Salvati and Michael Blasdell.

Representing the Long Beach Times during a Martin Luther King Day Celebration, Long Beach, California.

PUAA Country Development Director Michael Blasdell and his Excellency Chhoeung Namroven, Secretary of State the Royal Cambodian Government during the PUAA licensing ceremony.

United States Senator Olympia Snowe and Oni

The tree in the courtyard of Ta Probm Temple at Angkor Wat the second wonder in the world, where I had my vision for the future of Cambodia.

Fresh Face of Hope

The future of Cambodia depends on the economic, education, free society and health care of its children.

Oni Vitandham was born in a jungle cave in the Kompong Speu province of Cambodia, southwest of Phnom Penh, in 1972. Now an American citizen and living in Long Beach, California with her daughter, Reachiny. She works hard every single day to fulfill what she believes to be her destiny—to help other refugees like herself and to prevent the same horrors from happening to the children of Cambodia ever again. In 1995 she founded the Progressive United Action Association, now known as PUAA, the Foundation for Cambodia, a non-profit organization dedicated to ending social injustice in Cambodia and enriching the lives of Cambodian children through education of HIV/AIDS and humanitarian relief. Oni is also a songwriter with two CDs on the way. This is her first book and Oni is currently working on her second book.

Order more copies of this book at

TATE PUBLISHING, LLC

127 East Trade Center Terrace
Mustang, OK 73064

(888)361 - 9473

Tate Publishing, LLC

www.tatepublishing.com